THE STORY OF
THE WORLD
BOOK III
The Awakening
of Europe

MARGART B. SYNGE

E.M. SYNGE, ILLUSTRATOR

COSIMOCLASSICS

NEW YORK

THE STORY OF THE WORLD - BOOK III
Cover © 2007 Cosimo, Inc.

For information, address:

Cosimo, P.O. Box 416
Old Chelsea Station
New York, NY 10113-0416

or visit our website at:
www.cosimobooks.com

THE STORY OF THE WORLD - BOOK III
was originally published in 1904.

Cover design by www.kerndesign.net

ISBN: 978-1-60206-622-9

Was there a sailor daring enough to sail over the mysterious north pole itself to reach the other side? Yes. Henry Hudson was willing to try. And in a tiny ship, with a scanty crew, he sailed away on his adventurous voyage to the frozen seas. A fortnight later he reached Greenland.

—from *The Awakening of Europe*

CONTENTS.

THE AWAKENING OF EUROPE.

1. STORY OF THE NETHERLANDS.

"God made the sea, but the Hollander made the land."
—*Old Dutch Proverb.*

FAR away, in the north-west corner of Europe, lie
the Netherlands, the lands which are now to play
a large part in the world's history. The Low
Countries they were called by the men of old time;
and with good reason too, for many parts were
actually below the level of the sea. Spongy and
marshy, bleak and cold, was this corner of the
European continent in the olden days.

Winds and waves had wrought sad havoc with
the coast. The rough North Sea was ever en-
croaching on the low-lying land, breaking over the
shores with its never-ceasing roar and tumble, and
flooding the country below its level whenever the
wild west wind blew it home. Not only had the
people of this country to contend with wind and

wave, but from the other side many great rivers
rolled through the land, to empty their waters into
the North Sea, overflowing their low banks and
flooding the surrounding neighbourhood.

The largest of these was the Rhine.   Rising
amid the snowy Alps, leaping joyously over the
famous falls of Schaffhausen, flowing in majesty
right through Germany, the Rhine at last reached
the Netherlands.   The mouth of this famous river
gave some trouble to the Hollanders.   They made
colossal pumps and locks, by which they lifted the
water and lowered it into the sea.   There was no
rest for a lazy river in these parts.   The stream
must be kept moving, it must do its share of work
in the country.

"As long as grass grows and water runs."   This
was their idea of For ever.

"I struggle but I emerge."

This was the motto of Zeeland, with the crest
of a lion riding out of the waves, and it sums
up the story of the people of the Netherlands.
For hundreds of years they fought the angry
waters with a stubborn determination, a patient
energy, a dauntless genius,—an example to other
countries.

They erected great mounds or dykes to keep
out the North Sea; they dug canals to direct the
course of their sluggish rivers and to keep them
within bounds.   And when the ocean tides were
high or the winds blew long from the west; when

the heavy snows from the mountains melted, or
the rainfall was unusually great, so that the dykes
were broken down and the waters rushed in bound-
less masses over their land, yet the Hollander
would not give up. With dogged perseverance he
began again, so that to-day such an inundation is
impossible.

"God made the sea, but we made the land,"
they can say to-day with pride. But even to-day
these great dykes which keep out the sea have to
be watched. Every little hole has to be carefully
stopped up or the sea would rush in and devour
the land once more. Every man, woman, and
child in the country knows the importance of
this.

A little Dutch boy was returning from school
in the late afternoon, with his bag of books
hanging over his shoulder, when he thought he
heard the sound of running water. He stood still
and listened. Like all other little boys in the
Netherlands, he knew that the least crack in a
dyke would soon let in the water, that it would
cover the land and bring ruin to the people. He
ran to the mound and looked about. There he saw
a small hole, through which the water had already
begun to trickle. He was some way from his home
yet. Suppose he were to run on fast and tell
some one to come. It might already be too late
—the water might even then be rushing over the
land. He stooped down on the cold damp ground

and put his fat little hand into the hole where the water was running out. It was just big enough to stop up the hole and prevent the water from escaping any more.

His mind was made up; he must stop there till some one came to relieve him. He grew cold and hungry, but no one passed that lonely way. The sun set, the night grew dark, and

The little Dutch boy and the dyke.

the cold winds began to blow. Still the little boy kept his hand in the hole. Hour after hour passed away, and he grew more and more cold and frightened as the night advanced. At last he saw little streaks of light across the sky; the dawn was coming. By-and-by the sun rose, and the boy knew his long lonely watch must soon be over. He was right. Some workmen going early to work found him crouched on the ground with his little cold hand still thrust into the hole. But the large tears were on his cheeks, and his piteous cries showed how hard he had found it to keep faithful all through the long dark night. The boy was at once set free and the hole was mended. And so it depends on each man to watch the dykes, though there are now bands of watchers appointed by the State for this purpose.

So these people have, as the poet says, "scooped out an empire" for themselves, and kept it by their never-ceasing vigilance and industry.

2. BRAVE LITTLE HOLLAND.

"Brave men are brave from the very first."
—CORNEILLE.

IT will be interesting to trace the history of these resolute people, who reclaimed their land from the angry North Sea and built busy cities which should play a large part in the history of the world.

The earliest chapter in the history of the Netherlands was written by their conqueror, Julius Cæsar.[1] Why he cast covetous eyes towards these swampy lowlands is hard to see, but he must needs conquer them, and he thought he should

[1] See Book I. chapter 50.

have an easy task. At least one tribe wrung from him admiration by its rare courage. When others were begging for mercy, these people swore to die rather than to surrender. At the head of ten Roman legions Cæsar advanced to the banks of one of the many rivers of this low country. But hardly had the Roman horsemen crossed the stream, when down rushed a party of Netherlanders from the summit of a wooded hill and overthrew horses and riders in the stream. For a moment it seemed as if this wild lowland tribe was going to conquer the disciplined forces of Rome. Snatching a shield, the world's conqueror plunged into the hottest of the fight and soon turned the tide. The battle was lost, but, true to their vow, the wild Netherlanders refused to surrender. They fought on till the ground was heaped with their dead—fought till they had perished almost to a man. Cæsar could respect such courage, and when he left the country, to be governed by Romans, he took back soldiers from the Netherlanders to form his imperial guard in Rome.

When in the fifth century the Romans sailed away from the shores of Britain to defend their own land, they turned their backs on the Netherlands.

Then came the "Wandering of the Nations,"[1] when barbarians from the north and west tramped

[1] See Book II. chapter 11.

over the country. This was followed by the dark ages, when the Netherlands with the rest of Europe was plunged in sleep.

Charlemagne [1] next arose and added the Netherlands to his great kingdom of the Franks. "Karel de Groote," as he was called, was very fond of this new part of his great possessions. He built himself a beautiful palace at Nimwegen, high up on a table-land raised above the surrounding country. For beauty of scenery he could hardly have chosen a more lovely spot. Below lay some of the many rivers, making their way slowly through the low country to the sea, while the rich meadows and fields beyond were the scenes of legend and poetry of a later age. At Nimwegen to-day the curfew rings at 8.30 every evening. It is often called Keizer Karel's Klok. In the city museum the dead world seems to live again in the relics of the past.

With the death of Karel de Groote came the Norsemen. Up the many creeks and into the rivers of the Netherlands these fierce Vikings [2] pushed their single-masted galleys. For three centuries they were a terror to every sea-coast country.

"From the fury of the Northmen, good Lord, deliver us," sobbed the men of the Netherlands with the rest of Europe.

For further protection the Netherlands were

[1] See Book II. chapter 14.   [2] See Book II. chapter 15.

divided up into provinces, each put under a count or lord. Among others was one, Count Dirk, who was set over the little province of Holland. It was a small piece of country along the sea-coast, but it was destined to be the cradle of an empire. And this is the first mention of Holland in history—the low land, the hollow land, as it was called. The Count of Holland lived at Haarlem till he built himself a castle to the south, standing some three miles from the sea. To make it safe it was surrounded by a hedge, known as the Count's Hedge—Graven Hage—now The Hague, the Capital of the Netherlands. Then the Counts of Holland also built the new town of Dordrecht. "Every ship that comes up the river shall pay toll for the new town," said Dirk. But this made the men of other provinces very angry, and the men of Friesland fought over it.

But a time was at hand when they should find something better to fight over than the toll of Dordrecht. The new teaching under the name of Christianity was making its way to the Netherlands, and the Counts of Holland were not slow to join the rest of Europe in their rush to the Holy Land, to free the Holy Sepulchre from the hands of the Mohammedans.[1]

One day the men from Holland sailed down the river Maas in twelve ships, gay with banners and streamers, and out into the North Sea, on

[1] See Book II. chapter 18.

their way to the Holy Land. They would have to sail down the English Channel, between the coasts of England and France, through the Bay of Biscay and the Straits of Gibraltar, to the eastern ports of the blue Mediterranean, before ever they could reach their destination. But it is probable that the Crusades did more for Holland than Holland did for the Crusades, for by her contact with the East she learnt that of which she had not even dreamt before.

3. A WEALTH OF HERRINGS.

"Commerce changes the fate and genius of nations."
—T. GRAY.

IT has been said that the Crusades did more for the Netherlands than perhaps the Netherlands did for the Crusades. Thousands of ignorant, half-civilised Hollanders left their cold wet homes in the north to feast their eyes on the sunny land of Syria.

From their huts and rude lives they came into contact with great cities, such as Constantinople and Alexandria. They saw houses of marble and Greek statues; they met men of learning and scholars of Greece and Rome. For the first time they saw the use of linen sheets, carpets, soap, and spices. All the refinement and luxury of the East, the golden sunshine, the

brilliant dresses, came before the Hollanders and
dazzled them—after their dull lives and overcast
climate.

They returned home full of new wants. They,
too, must have linen sheets and pillow-cases; they,
too, must make their food pleasant with the spices
of the East. They must build more ships to send
round to Venice; they must trade by the over-
land route to the Queen of the Adriatic, and establish
closer relations with the East.

Changes, too, passed over the landscape of
Holland. The idea of the windmill was brought
back from the East. To make their rough winds
work, as they blew over the flat land, commended
itself to the Hollanders, and very soon hundreds
of windmills were working all over the country.
To-day they stand in thousands, like sentinels
keeping guard over the land. Not only do they
pump water, but they saw wood, grind grain, help
to load and unload the boats and hoist burdens.
Just as the lazy rivers were made to work, so the
wind has been made to do its share too. And these
mills played a very large part in the commerce that
at this time arose in the Netherlands.

It was natural that a people living in constant
conflict with the sea should seek their livelihood
in fishing and spend much of their time on the
water. From the earliest times they were a seafaring people. "Holland is an island," wrote an
old historian, "inhabited by a brave and warlike

people, who have never been conquered by their neighbours and who prosecute their commerce on every sea."

So the Hollanders built their ships, and fished their creeks and inlets, and did a thriving trade in herrings.

Early in the fourteenth century there lived a man called Beukels. He was unknown and poor, but he made a great discovery, which did much to enrich his country. He found out how to keep herrings by curing them, so that they could be packed in barrels and exported. Herrings were a very valuable food in those days, when the Church demanded much fasting for her members. For a long time the Hollanders kept the herring-fishing to themselves. They sailed across to the British coasts opposite and fished in the bays and inlets of Scotland, and they became rich.

"The foundations of Amsterdam are laid on herring-bones," they used to say of one of their most wealthy towns. So herring-fishery helped to lay the foundation of the wealth of the Netherlands.

But there were soon other sources of wealth. Flax was brought back from Egypt and grown in Holland, until Dutch flax became famous all over Europe. Linen-factories sprang up. Tablecloths, shirts, handkerchiefs, were manufactured. For a long time linen sheets, pillow - cases, and shirts were used only by kings and nobles. They were rough and dark-coloured; but the Dutch studied

the art of bleaching, till all over Europe the "finest
linen, white as snow," was known as holland.   The
ground around Haarlem was used largely for this
process of bleaching or spreading out the sheets
of linen in the sun, till the country looked as if a
snowstorm had whitened the earth.

The wool trade, carried on chiefly in the south
of the Netherlands, was a source of power, and
the Flemish weavers were famous throughout
Europe.   The towns of Ghent and Bruges had
long been centres of importance ; they were among
the richest towns in Europe.   From foreign lands
came raw material to be made up here.   Every year
the famous "Northern Squadron" from Venice
visited the neighbourhood ; it was the great
market-place of English wool, and thrived until
that day when Vasco da Gama found the route
to India by the Cape of Good Hope.   Then, with
Venice, the famous cities of Ghent and Bruges
fell.

"Grass grew in the fair and pleasant streets
of Bruges, and seaweed clustered about the marble
halls of Venice."

The next city to rise to great importance was
Antwerp, which soon became the commercial capital not only of the Netherlands, but of the whole
world.   This was under Charles V., one of the
greatest figures in the early part of the sixteenth
century, whom it will be interesting now to
know.

4. A DUTCH REFORMER.

"Erasmus laid the egg and Luther hatched it."—Old Monks of the Reformation.

THE Netherlands now became absorbed in the greater kingdom of Charles V., who ruled over the largest empire since the days of Charlemagne. He was the grandson of that Ferdinand and Isabella of Spain who had driven the Moors from Granada[1] and sent Columbus on his great voyage to the New World. From his father he inherited the Netherlands, and in the year 1519 he was elected Emperor over the heads of the Kings of France and England, both claimants for the high position. His reign was full of importance, not only for the Netherlands, but for the whole world; for a wonderful change was passing over Europe — that great Renaissance,[2] at which we have already glanced for a moment. The new learning was spreading rapidly now, and the great empire of this Charles V. was not behindhand to adopt it. Indeed Holland was to produce one of the greatest scholars of the age in Erasmus, the forerunner of Martin Luther, the famous German Reformer.

"I have given up my whole soul to Greek learning," said this man in the early days of his

---

[1] See Book II. chapter 36.   [2] See Book II. chapter 52.

enthusiasm, "and as soon as I get any money I shall buy Greek books, and then I shall buy some clothes."

Erasmus was born at Rotterdam, one of the famous towns of the Netherlands at this time, in the year 1467, seven years after the death of the sailor Prince of Portugal.[1] He was a bright little boy with flaxen hair, grey-blue eyes, and with the voice of an angel.

"This little fellow will come to something by-and-by," said a famous scholar, patting the boy's flaxen head; for he had been struck with the ability of Erasmus as he inspected the school where he was learning. The boy had a passion for study. He devoured any book he could get hold of. He was always at work, writing poetry or essays; always thinking and pondering, though full of life and brightness. But monastery life was distasteful to him, and at the age of twenty he was glad to escape to Paris, still wearing his monk's dress, to continue his studies. He yearned to go to Italy, the centre of the new learning; to mix with the great Greek scholars; to breathe in the new life, which had not as yet taken root in his own country. But money was not forthcoming for this, and he made his way to England, where the new learning had been well received.

"I have found in Oxford," he soon wrote, "so

[1] See Book II. chapter 27.

much polish and learning that now I hardly care about going to Italy at all. When I listen to my friend Colet, it seems like listening to Plato himself."

Amid a little group of English scholars Erasmus found the sympathy he needed. Still he worked on at Greek translations, and wrote a new grammar-book for the little scholars under the new learning. Moreover, he gained some repute by writing a song of triumph over the old world of darkness and ignorance, which was to vanish away before the light and knowlege of the new era.

But more than this. He had studied his Bible very deeply and carefully, specially the New Testament and the writings of the early Fathers. He was greatly struck with the difference between the teaching of Christ by His disciples in the old days of long ago, and the distorted version of Christianity now taught by the priests, monks, and clergy of Europe. The people knew only what they were taught by the priests. Copies of the Bible were rare, shut up in convent libraries, and read only by the few. Erasmus saw that before any reform could take place the Bible must be in the hands of all, rich and poor alike.

"I wish that even the weakest woman might read the Gospels and the Epistles of St Paul," he says as he works during the long hours at his translation and notes. "I long for the day when the husbandman shall sing portions of them to himself as he follows the plough, when the weaver shall hum them to the tune of his shuttle, when the travellers shall while away with their stories the weariness of the journey."

Since his boyhood printing-presses had been established everywhere. At last his work was finished, text and translation printed, and the wonderful story of Christ, His disciples and His teaching, was revealed to an astonished world in all its beautiful simplicity.

"A single candle shone far in the universal darkness."

The New Testament of Erasmus became the topic of the day; every household eagerly purchased a copy; it was read and discussed with alternate fear and joy. A new era was dawning. Erasmus had sown the seeds of that more far-reaching movement which Martin Luther was to finish. He had prepared the way; but a greater than he was needed to stand up boldly, with the eyes of Europe on him, to denounce the abuses that had crept into the Christian teaching, and to show mankind the Christ of the New Testament.

5. THE STORY OF MARTIN LUTHER.

"The whole world and its history was waiting for this man."
—CARLYLE.

ERASMUS was sixteen years old when Martin
Luther was born,—Martin Luther, the great German Reformer, whose name was soon to be known
throughout the whole continent of Europe. This
is the story of his life. He was born in the year
1483. His father was a humble miner, his mother
was noted for her goodness and virtue. When
quite a little child, his parents wished to make a
"scholar" of him—so he was early taught to read
and write, and at six years old he was sent to
school. Both at home and at school his training
was very severe; his father whipped him for mere
trifles, and one day poor little Martin was beaten
fifteen times! He was bright and clever, but he
had a strong will of his own, and a love of fun
and mischief. When he was fourteen his parents
could not afford to keep him any longer, so they
sent him forth into the world with his bag on his
back, to seek for learning from the charity of
strangers. With a boy friend he set forth to walk
to Magdeburg, where there was a school for poor
boys kept by the Franciscan monks. In order to
get food on the way, the boys had to beg or to
sing. They were thankful enough for a morsel of

BK. III.   B

bread or a night's shelter. Indeed, life became such a hard struggle, that Martin told himself he would never be a scholar, and it would be better to return home and win an honest livelihood with his spade. But at this moment the tide turned. By his sweet voice he attracted the notice of a good lady, who took pity on him and gave him a comfortable home. Here he worked hard, making great progress in Latin, till he was eighteen. By this time his father had made enough money to send him to a university, where he took his degree in 1505.

And now a strange thing happened, that altered his whole life. One day he was walking with a friend, when a tremendous thunderstorm came on. A sudden vivid flash of lightning struck the friend at his side, who fell down dead at his feet. The suddenness of the young man's death made a great impression on Martin Luther. Struck to the heart, he made up his mind that henceforth he would devote his life to God and God's service. In spite of his father's protests he became a monk. For the first two years his life was a very hard one : his food was very scanty, he had to perform the lowliest tasks, and to beg for alms and bread. Whatever spare time he had, he worked hard at his books, studying the epistles and gospels diligently. In the library of the university he found a complete Bible in Latin. It was the first time he had seen one. He de-

voured it eagerly. A new light came into his
life, and in his close study of the Bible he
strengthened himself for his future work. Before
long he had risen to a position of importance in
the monastery. He became a priest and went
to live at Wittenberg—a town which he made
famous by his name. In 1509 he began to lecture
on the Scriptures. Bibles were not in the hands
of all as they are to-day, and Martin Luther was
able to tell his countrymen a great deal that
they did not know, by reason of his deep learning. His lectures made a great impression.

"This monk," said the head of the university,
"will bring in a new doctrine."

He also began now to preach in the churches.
He was very earnest, and the people who listened
to him were deeply moved at his words.

In 1511 he was sent on a mission to Rome,
where Leo X. was Pope. Now, from early times
there has been a Pope (*Papa*) or Father of Rome,
who in the Middle Ages had come to be looked on
as the Head of the Christian Church by many, if
not all, of the countries of Europe. At first the
Pope was a Bishop of Rome, as other Bishops were
in other cities, but when Rome was no longer the
sole imperial city, the power of the Bishops became
greater and greater until, in the twelfth century,
under Innocent III., the papal authority reached
its height.

Now during the Middle Ages many abuses had

crept into the Church. One of these was known as the "sale of indulgences."

All feel it right that sinners should suffer for their sins, but there is no Biblical foundation for the teaching that by money payments a sinner may be saved from the punishment of his sin. Yet, in those days, persons who paid money received an "indulgence," and agents went about the country selling them.

One of these, named John Tetzel, came to Germany. He disgusted Martin Luther by his methods of extorting money from ignorant people, and being a man of great courage, Luther felt it his duty to remonstrate. He stood up boldly in his pulpit and denounced the system openly.

It was a tremendous moment. It was indeed the visible beginning of the Reformation — that great movement which was to spread wider and wider until it should affect the whole Christian world.

Into the deeper causes of the Reformation we cannot enter here. The revival of Greek learning had caused men to study the Scriptures for themselves as Luther did, and this caused dissatisfaction with the mediæval corruption of the Roman Church.

6. THE DIET OF WORMS.

"Here stand I. I cannot act otherwise. So help me God!"
—Martin Luther.

Tetzel was coming to Wittenberg in the autumn of 1517 when Luther determined on more open opposition. It was the eve of All Saints when he posted up on the door of the church ninety-five reasons against the sale of indulgences. He had no idea what a storm he was raising. He did not wish to quarrel with the Pope, only to expose this abuse in the Church. But he had kindled the spark that fired the great Reformation. Widespread excitement followed, and at last Luther was summoned to Rome to answer for his ninety-five reasons. But the distance was great, and it was agreed that he should go to Augsburg, where a representative of the Pope would meet him.

Martin Luther was but a poor friar still, and he walked the distance, clad in his brown frock with his few wants on his back. His fellow-citizens attended him to the gates and followed him some way along the road.

"Luther for ever!" they cried as they bade him farewell.

"No," he answered quietly, "Christ for ever!"

Arrived at Augsburg, the cardinal sent by the Pope received Luther with all civility. He made no doubt that he could soon settle this son of a German miner; and so perhaps he might, had he been the right man. But he took a high hand, and simply told him to withdraw his opposition and retract his words at once.

"What is wrong?" asked Luther.

The cardinal refused to discuss matters.

"I am come to command, not to argue," he replied.

But the little monk refused to retract.

Then, history says, the cardinal grew angry.

"What!" he cried. "What! Do you think the Pope cares for the opinion of a German peasant? The Pope's little finger is stronger than all Germany. Do you expect princes to defend you. I tell you, No; and where will you be then?"

"Then, as now, in the hands of Almighty God," answered Luther.

Then cardinal and monk parted. But Luther was too deeply moved to keep silent.

"God hurries and drives me," he said. "I am not master of myself. I wish to be quiet and am hurried into the midst of tumults."

At this moment Charles V. became Emperor of Germany and ruler of half the world. Matters were now referred to him, for Luther was taking firmer ground and attacking not only the abuses of the papacy, but the whole Church of Rome.

At last a command came from the Pope forbid-

ding Luther to preach any more. He replied by
burning the document at the gate of the city.
Crowds gathered to see the fire blaze up. Then
Luther, pale as death, stepped forward holding
in his hand the document with the Pope's seal
upon it. He knew full well what he was doing
now as he dropped it into the flames that rose
high that wintry afternoon at Wittenberg. The
crowds shouted approval and admiration.

"It was the shout of the awakening of nations,"
says a famous writer. Not only the little crowd
at Wittenberg, but the whole world, was looking
on. For that little fire lit up the whole of Europe.
Luther was now ordered by the Emperor Charles
to appear before a council, or Diet, as it was called,
which should meet at Worms, a city on the Rhine.
He was warned by his friends not to go, for feeling
ran high. There would surely be bloodshed, they
told him, and he would never leave Worms alive.

"Were there as many devils in Worms as there
are tiles upon the roofs of the houses, I would go
on," replied Luther.

The whole country was moved by his heroism.
Whether he was right or whether he was wrong,
this was a brave man. In April 1521, at ten in
the morning, he arrived at Worms in the covered
waggon provided for him.

"God will be with me," he said as he descended
from the waggon.

Crowds assembled to see him as he passed to

the council chamber, this resolute little monk, who
was defying the Pope of Rome.

Inside, the scene was most impressive. On a
raised platform sat Charles V., ruler of half the
world. Archbishops, ministers, princes, stood on
either side to hear and judge this son of a miner
who had made the world ring with his name. In
the body of the hall stood knights and nobles, stern
hard men in gleaming armour. Between them
Luther was led, still in his monk's dress. As he
passed up the hall a knight touched him on the
arm.

"Pluck up thy spirit, little monk," he said.
"Some of us here have seen warm work in our
time, but never knight in this company more
needed a stout heart than thou needest it now.
If thou hast faith, little monk, go on ; in the name
of God, forward !"

"Yes," said Luther, throwing back his head, " in
the name of God, forward !"

At last he stood alone before his judges. "It
was the greatest scene in modern European history
—the greatest moment in the modern history of
men."

The books he had written lay on a table at hand.
The titles were read aloud, and he was asked if he
had written them.

"Yes," was his firm answer.

Would he withdraw all he had written ? No—
that was impossible. For two long hours Luther

defended his opinions.   He would retract nothing. They might kill him if they wished, and he knew death was the penalty, but he was ready to die in such a cause.   What he said he now repeated, for the matter had gone far beyond the sale of indulgences by this time.

"Here stand I.   I cannot act otherwise.   So help me God!"

Uttering these famous words, he ended.

The council broke up in excitement, and Luther was free to go home.

"It is past! it is past!" he cried in heartrending accents, as he clasped his hands above his head.

The verdict was not long in coming.   It was against him.   He must preach no more, teach no more.   The emperor of half the world must uphold the authority of the Pope.

"Be it so," said Luther, uncomplaining.   "I will bear anything for his Imperial Majesty and the Empire, but the Word of God must not be bound."

For the next year he was sheltered by one of his friends in an old German castle, lest he should suffer violence from the hands of those who disapproved his conduct.   But after a time he returned to Wittenberg,—the scene of his old labours, —while others carried on the work of reformation which he had begun.

7. AN HISTORIC SCENE.

"Europe's eye is fixed on mighty things,
  The fall of empires and the fate of kings."
                 —BURNS.

THE great movement known as the Reformation
now swept through Europe. Gradually the conflict, begun in Germany between Luther and the
Pope, passed into England, Scotland, Sweden,
Denmark, and the Netherlands. Throughout the
long vexed reign of the Emperor Charles V. this
war of religion raged fiercely, intolerantly. Those
who followed Luther were known as the Protestants, or those who protested against the power
of the Pope, while those who acknowledged the
supreme power of Rome were Roman Catholics.

In the year 1530 a religious peace was made at
Augsburg. Though Martin Luther was not allowed
to appear, he helped to draw up twenty-eight
articles of the faith professed by the Protestants.

Luther passed to his rest, but his followers carried on the conflict. Twenty-six years after the
Diet of Worms Charles the emperor was at Wittenberg. He asked to see the tomb of Martin Luther.
As he stood gazing at it, full of many thoughts,
some one suggested that the body should be taken
up, tied to a stake, and burned in the market-
place of the town. There was nothing unusual in

the suggestion. Most heretics were burned in those days. They thought to please the emperor, but Charles was "one of nature's gentlemen."

"I war not with the dead," he answered quietly.

But the troubles and toils of a long reign had already begun to tell on the emperor, and he determined to lay down a burden which he was no longer fitted to bear. The 25th of October 1555 was fixed for the great abdication of this mighty emperor. It was to take place in the palace at Brussels, the Court residence of the emperor in the Netherlands. His beloved son Philip was to succeed him.

Long before the appointed hour crowds had filled the historic palace. The wealth of the Netherlands was there. There were the knights of the famous Order of the Golden Fleece; there was the flower of Flemish chivalry—bishops, counts, barons, representatives from all the emperor's vast empire. As the clock struck three the hero of the whole scene arrived. "Cæsar," as he was more often called, in the classic language of the day, came in leaning heavily on the shoulder of William of Orange, the man who was to play such a large part in the story of the Netherlands. They were followed by Philip, and accompanied by an immense throng of glittering Spanish warriors. Here stood Count Egmont, the idol of the people, whose victories were to resound through Europe, tall, gallant, ill-fated. Here, too, was Count Horn, sullen and gloomy, though as yet ignorant of his coming tragedy.

The whole company rose to their feet as the emperor entered, and all eyes were directed towards him and his young son. Charles himself, though not yet fifty-six, was bent with old age, crippled with gout, worn with anxiety. It was with some difficulty that he supported himself even with the aid of a crutch. Philip, his son, had the same broad forehead and blue eyes of his father; but he was very small, with thin legs, a narrow chest, and the timid air of an invalid. He had been married but a year since to Mary of England, a valuable alliance to this great empire which was now passing into his weak hands.

Presently the emperor rose, supporting himself upon the shoulder of a handsome young man of two-and-twenty. Then he spoke to the vast throng before him. He sketched shortly his wars, his nine expeditions into Germany, six to Spain, seven to Italy, four to France, two to England, ten to the Netherlands, two to Africa, and eleven voyages by sea. He assured his subjects that he had striven to uphold the Roman Catholic religion. They knew of his lifelong opposition to Martin Luther. Now he told them life was ebbing away. Instead of an old man whose strength was past, they should have a young man in the prime of his youthful manhood to rule over them. Turning to the fair-haired son at his side, he bequeathed to him the magnificent empire, begging him to prove himself worthy of so great an inheritance. He entreated the nations under him to help in the colossal task of putting down the Protestants in the empire; then, beseeching them to pardon his own shortcomings, he ceased.

Sobs were heard in every part of the hall, and tears flowed from many eyes, as the old emperor sank back, pale and fainting, into his golden chair. The tears poured freely down his furrowed cheeks as Philip dropped on his knees and kissed his hand with reverence. Raising his son, he kissed him tenderly.

So the curtain fell for ever upon the mightiest emperor since the days of Charlemagne, and when it rose again Philip had begun the long and tremendous tragedy which lasted till his death.

8. HOW THE TROUBLE BEGAN.

"Our noisy years seem moments in the being
  Of the Eternal Silence."
                              —WORDSWORTH.

PHILIP was now left to gather up the reins of his mighty empire, keeping ever in view the desire of his father to crush the Protestants out of the land. Nowhere had they increased more rapidly than in the Netherlands. The first Dutch Bible had been

printed some thirty years before this time, at
Amsterdam, but the study of it had been for-
bidden by the emperor under pain of death.

"And if you will not obey me, you shall be
burned," he added.

Two monks were burned at once for disobeying
the royal command—the first Protestant martyrs
of the Netherlands, the leaders of a great host
who were afterwards burnt at the stake for conscience' sake. Still the numbers of Luther's followers increased. A further step was taken.

Men called Inquisitors were sent by the emperor
to question the people about their belief, with
instructions to burn alive all those who took part
with Luther against the Pope. But, as in the
days of the early Christians in Rome, the martyr-
dom of the Protestants only tended to strengthen
their faith. Hundreds and thousands had been
burnt in the Netherlands under the Emperor
Charles. It was not likely that Philip would be
more tolerant. To begin with, he had no sympathy with the Netherlands. Born and educated
in Spain, he was Spanish to the backbone, and his
great idea was to make Spain the capital of his
empire, so that he might rule from there. So,
four years after his accession, he made his sister
Margaret Regent of the Netherlands, and sailed
away from Flushing for sunny Spain, never to
return.

"I shall not rest so long as there is one man

left believing in the teaching of Martin Luther," he said as he left his sister to carry out his instructions. And the Inquisition went forward more rigidly than ever before.

But no sooner had Philip turned his back than the men of the Netherlands began to show their discontent. Spanish soldiers had been left behind to enforce the Inquisition; day by day men were dragged from their homes, tortured, and killed for reading the Bible in Dutch, or for listening to Protestant teaching. In their misery many of them went to England, where they were kindly treated, and where there never was any Inquisition.

Meanwhile Margaret saw the growing frenzy of the people, and grew alarmed. She was a rigid Roman Catholic herself, but she saw that her brother was pushing things too far in the Netherlands. She wrote despairing letters to him, describing the gloomy state of the country and her fears of a rebellion. She sent the Count Egmont in person to try and alarm him as to the serious state of affairs.

But nothing was done. At last the nobles of the land determined to intercede. Some 200 of them made their way to the abode of Margaret in Brussels with a petition. An immense crowd watched them with shouts and cheers, for were they not the deliverers of the land from the tyranny of the Spanish Inquisition? They passed through the great hall where ten years before

Charles had abdicated his throne, and entered the council-chamber. The document was read to Margaret. It told her what she already knew, but it affected her deeply, and at the end she remained quite silent with tears raining down her cheeks.

"Is it possible that your highness is afraid of these Beggars?" cried one standing by her. "Take my advice and you will drive them faster down the steps of the palace than they came up."

Begun in a jest, the name of Beggars became the watchword of these men, the famous cry of liberty, which was to ring over land and sea, amid burning cities, on blood-stained decks, through the smoke and din of many a battlefield. They dressed themselves in the beggar's garb of coarse grey, they wore the beggar's wallet and common felt caps, while each wore a newly made badge with the words, "Faithful to the King, even to the beggar's sack." They shaved off their beards to resemble beggars yet more nearly. Hundreds of Netherlanders now became Beggars, until they became as "numerous as the sands on the sea-shore."

"Long live the Beggars!" cried the people, until Margaret grew more and more alarmed at their gathering numbers and their defiant air. And still her brother Philip was blind to the coming danger.

"You have done wrong," he wrote to her. "We will not be less cruel to the Protestants. I will not give up the Inquisition."

9. THE STORM BURSTS.

"Like one fierce cloud over a waste of waves
Hung Tyranny."
—SHELLEY.

THE answer from Philip had come, but a more terrible one was to follow. The news soon spread through the already heart-broken Netherlands, that the Duke of Alva was on his way with a splendid Spanish army, to suppress in the country the struggle for religious liberty. All knew what this meant. Alva's name was known and feared throughout Europe. Like his royal master, he would have no mercy, no pity on the Netherlands. He had come to conquer, not to make peace.

"I have tamed men of iron in my day," he had said with contempt; "shall I not easily crush these men of butter?"

The whole country shuddered at the arrival of this man, as they prepared, almost hopelessly, to defend their religious liberty to the end. Alva's first act was to get rid of the Counts Egmont and Horn, who, though rigid Roman Catholics, had openly showed their disgust at the cruelty and injustice of the Inquisition. Professing great friendship for them, he invited them both to his house in Brussels one evening to talk over the plans—so he said—of a great castle he meant to build in Antwerp. The counts went, though they

had been warned of treachery. A large plan of
the proposed castle lay on the table, and the counts
discussed it warmly with Alva. Suddenly Alva,
feigning illness, left the room. Not long after,
the party broke up. ·The Count Horn had left,
and Egmont was leaving, when he was requested
to stay behind a moment. Then a Spanish soldier
ordered him to give up his sword; others rushed
in, and he was hurried to a dark room with barred
windows and hung with black. Meanwhile the
Count Horn had been arrested outside, and both
were sent to a dungeon in the Castle of Ghent.

Having accomplished this, Alva next appointed
a council of men to help him in carrying out
the king's commands. This council is known to
history by the terrible name of the " Blood-Council,"
and so thoroughly did it perform its deadly work
that in three months 1800 human beings had
suffered death at its hands. Men, women, children,
were beheaded or burnt. There were stakes and
scaffolds in every village, every hour tolled the
church bells for one who had suffered in their
midst. It seemed as if the spirit of the nation
was broken, as if the suffering people could endure
no more.

Having been confined in the Castle of Ghent
for nearly a year, the Counts Egmont and Horn
were now brought up for trial before the Blood-
Council. They were found guilty and condemned to
die by the sword on the following day, their heads

to hang on high in some public place decreed by
Alva. He knew the death of the counts would
have a great effect on the people of the Netherlands.

It was a summer morning in the June of 1568.
Three thousand Spanish troops were drawn up
in battle array round the scaffold, which had been
set up in the large square at Brussels. Then Count
Egmont was led forth. He wore a robe of red
damask, over which was thrown a short black
mantle worked in gold, while on his head he wore
a black silk hat with plumes.

"Hear my cry, O God, and give ear unto my
prayer," he cried as he walked to his death.

He was beheaded together with his friend and
countryman, Count Horn. As Alva had foretold,
their deaths made a deep impression on the public
mind. If tears fell from the eyes of the Netherlanders, they also fell from those of the Spanish
soldiers, who had respected the counts as brave
and valiant generals. It is said, too, that tears
were even seen on the iron cheek of Alva, who
was gazing at the ghastly scene from a window
opposite. But from that hour the people hated
Alva with a more bitter hatred than before. The
death of such nobles of high birth filled the land
with horror and anguish. They determined never
to rest till they had overthrown the power of Spain.

Alva was now Governor-General of the Netherlands, and Margaret had left the country for ever.

10. BEGGARS OF THE SEA.

"Long live the Beggars! Christians, ye must cry.
Long live the Beggars! pluck up courage then.
Long live the Beggars! if ye would not die.
Long live the Beggars! shout, ye Christian men."
—*Beggar's Song* (1570).

THE story of the fight of the Netherlands for liberty now becomes more or less the story of one man's life. That man was William of Orange, or William the Silent, as he was called from his quiet ways. It was on his shoulder that the broken-down old emperor had leant when, thirteen years before this, he had resigned his empire and returned to Spain, leaving Philip to manage his affairs.

William of Orange had been left in the Netherlands to rule over the provinces in the north—Holland, Zealand, Utrecht, and Friesland. He soon discovered Philip's plan of planting the Inquisition in the Netherlands, and from this time up to the last tragic moment of his life he toiled to suppress it and to uphold the ancient rights and liberties of his country. From this time he came forward to champion the cause of the Netherlands. He was to prove, indeed, the "guiding-star of a whole brave nation." Of him it would be truly said, that he went through life "bearing the load of a people's sorrows upon his shoulders with a smiling face."

"Tranquil amid raging waves," was the motto of his life. And perhaps no man ever carried out their life's decree more completely than did this man, William the Silent.

He had been born in Germany and brought up as a follower of Luther, but Charles V. had carried him off to Spain and educated him as a Roman Catholic. When Philip introduced the Inquisition and burnt people for their opinions, William grew very thoughtful. He thought that Christians of every kind should live together in peace, and for this end he worked in a cruel age, which could not understand so high a creed. The result of his own deep thought, combined with all that had passed, was, that he returned to the belief of his boyhood, and enrolled himself for ever a soldier of the Reformation.

William had been in Germany, when his friends the Counts Egmont and Horn had been led forth to die in the square at Brussels, raising troops for his brothers to march against the Duke of Alva. But they had fought in vain. They were no match for the brilliant Spanish commander and his well-trained troops.

Unsuccessful by land, William, undaunted, turned his eyes to the sea. The men of the Netherlands were more at home on the sea, after all; they had always been sailors and fishermen, and every sea-coast city had its ships. They would chase the Spaniard by sea and destroy the ships sailing to

ruin their fair country.   So the "Sea Beggars,"
as they were called, began their wild work, sailing
over the high seas, living as the old Vikings had
done, by pillage and plunder.

One day—it was the 1st of April—they were
coasting about the mouth of the Meuse, when they
found they had eaten all their food.   There were
some 300 of them at most, and they must land
in order to avert starvation.   The little seaport
town of Briel, or The Brille, lies near the mouth
of the broad river Meuse.   It was known to be in
the hands of the Duke of Alva, like the rest of
the country, at this time; but the Sea Beggars
were hungry, the Sea Beggars were also desperate.
So about two o'clock on this April afternoon a
ferryman from Briel saw the squadron sailing up
the broad mouth of the river towards Briel.   He
at once gave the alarm that the Sea Beggars were
here, though secretly the stout-hearted ferryman
was in sympathy with the marauders.

The inhabitants of Briel were struck with terror.
" How many of the Sea Beggars were coming ? "

" There might be some 5000," carelessly answered
the ferryman.   The Spaniards and townspeople
decided to take refuge in flight.   They sent two
men to confer with the strangers, while they fled
from the town.   So the Sea Beggars entered the
deserted town of Briel, and the admiral took
lawful possession of it in the name of William of
Orange.

It was the first step in the freedom of Holland,
and it was achieved by some 250 wild seamen
driven from their country by Spanish rulers.

"Up with Orange!" was the cry henceforth
wrung from the very hearts of the stricken
people.

The hero prince should yet come to his own
again. The first ray of light had penetrated the
gloom of years, and all hands were now stretched
out to William the Silent, who should yet save
their country.

And while the rage of the Duke of Alva knew
no bounds, the men of Holland sang aloud in their
joy the popular couplet—

> "On April Fools' Day
> Duke Alva's spectacles [1] were stolen away."

11. THE MASSACRE OF ST BARTHOLOMEW.

"'Twas pitiful, 'twas wondrous pitiful."—SHAKSPERE.

BUT the Netherlands was not the only place where
persecution for religion was going on. Though
Spain and the Netherlands lay paralysed under
the heavy hand of the Inquisition, yet France and
England were taking part, together with the rest
of Europe, in the struggle between Protestants
and Roman Catholics. And this very year, when

[1] *Brill* = spectacles (Dutch).

the Protestants seemed to be gaining ground in the Netherlands, France was to be stained with a crime which can never be forgotten, and which historians must always remember, as one of the greatest blots in the annals of mankind. This was the wholesale massacre of the Protestants, or Huguenots as they were called, in France, on a terrible summer night in the year 1572.

Francis, King of France, had left a delicate little brother to succeed him on the throne, and his mother, Catherine de Medici, was to govern the kingdom till the boy Charles was old enough and strong enough to rule it himself. She was a rigid Roman Catholic, and hated the Huguenots with her whole heart. Indeed, like her neighbour Philip over the Pyrenees, she made up her mind to crush them out of the country.

The leaders of the French Huguenots were the young Henry of Navarre and the Prince of Condé, and it was against these two that Catherine de Medici plotted. She planned a marriage between her daughter Margaret and young Henry of Navarre, the former being a Roman Catholic, the latter a Huguenot. It seemed strange to those who looked on, and men grew to suspect the motives of the Queen-Regent.

"We shall marry the two religions," said the young King of France, who was entirely under his mother's control.

Still, amid murmurs of discontent, the wedding

preparations went forward, until the day arrived for Henry, now King of Navarre, to come to Paris for his bride. Attended by the Prince of Condé, the old warrior Huguenot Admiral Coligny, and 800 distinguished followers, the King of Navarre rode into the French capital, his handsome face and winning smile attracting all alike. Still there were murmurs of disapproval, and the air was heavy with evil rumours.

The wedding-day came. It was the 18th of August, a glorious summer morning. Cannons roared, bells rang out from every steeple, crowds lined the street as King Henry, dressed in pale yellow satin adorned with silver and pearls, led out his young bride. It was a gorgeous sight. Bishops and archbishops led the way in robes of gold, cardinals in scarlet, knights blazing with orders, officers of State—all added to the splendour of the sight.

The next three days were spent in festivities. All seemed peace and goodwill. The young king, Charles IX., was making friends with the Admiral Coligny ; he already loved his new brother-in-law, Henry of Navarre. Catherine grew alarmed lest her plot should, after all, fail, and her own power over the young king should wane. She gave orders for the Admiral Coligny to be killed. Her commands were imperfectly carried out. The Admiral was badly wounded, but not killed. When Charles heard the news he was in an agony of surprise and fear. His mother was in a panic. Huguenots gathered in angry crowds and discussed the deed, Henry of Navarre vowed vengeance on the would-be murderer.

It was after dinner on the 23rd of August that Catherine led her son outside into the private gardens of the Tuileries to unfold her plan. The time, she said, was ripe. Eight thousand Huguenots were in Paris breathing revenge. In one hour the whole hated body of them might be put to death. To this the young king's sanction must be obtained. And first of all Coligny must be killed. Charles burst into one of his fits of passion.

"Woe to any one who touches a hair of his head!" he cried. "He is the only friend I have, save my brother of Navarre."

But Catherine would not give in. She knew she must conquer at last. And she did. Lashed into a frenzy, the young king started to his feet.

"Kill the Admiral, then, if you like!" he screamed; "but kill all the Huguenots with him —all—all—all, so that not one be left to reproach me with this deed."

The word was spoken. There was no time to lose. Hastily through the darkness of the starless summer night preparations went forward.

"Let every true Catholic tie a white band on his arm, put a white cross on his cap, and begin the vengeance of God," went forth the order.

Catherine de Medici planning the Massacre.

The signal was to be given by the great bell of the Palace of Justice at two o'clock in the morning. Soon after midnight Catherine went to her son. He was pacing his room in an agony of passion, swearing the Huguenots should not die.

" It is too late to retreat, even if it were possible," declared Catherine.

Feverishly mother and son awaited the signal. As the harsh sound of the bell rang through the silent summer night the uproar began. The sound of clanging bells, crashing doors, musket - shots, was followed by the shrieks of the victims and the yells of the crowd, till the stoutest hearts quailed and the strongest trembled. Shaking in every limb, the poor young king shouted for the massacre to be stopped. It was too late. Already beacon-fires had sent the signal through the land of France.

Old men, young girls, helpless children, were alike smitten down. Through the long dark night the slaughter continued, until Paris was such a scene of terror as human eyes have rarely seen.

In vain did Charles order the massacre to be stopped at the end of one day. It was continued for a whole week, till some 80,000 Huguenots had been slain.

And " the heart of Protestant Europe stood still with horror."

12. THE SIEGE OF LEYDEN.

"Better a drowned land than a lost land."
—MOTLEY.

THE news of the terrible massacre of St Bartholomew that had staggered Europe seemed only to strengthen the resolution of the Protestants in the Netherlands. The return of William of Orange had given new vigour to the Hollanders; town after town rose after the taking of Briel, turned out the hated Spaniard, and raised aloft the colours of their Prince. As winter came on and the great expanses of water froze into masses of solid ice, the undaunted Dutchmen put on their skates and glided into battle, to the astonishment of the Spaniards. Not to be beaten, Alva ordered 7000 pairs of skates to be supplied to the Spaniards, who soon became expert skaters too.

Haarlem was now attacked—Haarlem, one of the most beautiful cities in the country, lying between the Zuyder Zee and the German Ocean. With the utmost heroism she held out for seven months and then fell. She had cost the Spaniards 12,000 men; and even rich Spain, with all her treasure from the New World, could not go on much longer at this rate.

Men from England were helping the Netherlands

now. Over the seas they sailed in small companies, and with pike and musket they stood shoulder to shoulder with the men of Haarlem against the power of mighty Spain.

"Like a hen calling her chickens, his Majesty still seeks to gather you all under the parental wing," cried Alva at last. "But if you will not," he added sternly, "every city in the Netherlands shall be burned to the ground."

The Protestants refused, and the Spaniards next besieged the town of Leyden, to the south of Haarlem. It was one of the most wonderful feats of the whole war.

The siege began on October 1573. It was October 1574 when it ended, and all through this long dreary year the Dutchmen inside the town were fighting with famine and starvation—fighting for their religious liberty and freedom from the Spanish tyranny.

In the very centre of Leyden rose an old tower, standing high above the surrounding low country. From it could be seen the broad fertile fields which once had lain under the sea, little villages with their bright gardens and fruitful orchards, numerous canals, and the 145 bridges that spanned those watery streets.

The Prince of Orange was doing all he could from outside to help his countrymen in their plucky defence; but as the long months wore on their condition became desperate. They were starving, but they would not yield; for if Leyden fell, Holland fell too. Yet what could be done?

The Prince of Orange knew what could be done. "Better a drowned land than a lost land. If nothing else could save the city, the dykes could be opened, and the great stormy sea would once more ebb and flow over the country. Holland would be ruined, but it would not be in the hands of the Spaniards.

"We have held out as long as we can," wrote the starving citizens. "Human strength can do no more."

Then the Prince went himself and had the great dykes bored in sixteen places; the water-gates were opened, and the water began slowly to pour over the flat land.

The good news was carried into the despairing city. The citizens took fresh heart. Leyden, their city, would yet be saved. The besiegers, too, heard the news of the cutting of the dykes; but they did not believe in the possibility of the sea getting up so far as Leyden.

"Go up to the tower, ye Beggars," they laughed; "go up to the tower and tell us if you can see the ocean coming over the dry land to your relief."

And day after day the citizens crept up the old ruined tower and strained their eyes out over the sea, "watching, hoping, praying, fearing, and at last almost despairing of relief by God or man."

Meanwhile the Prince lay in a burning fever at

Rotterdam. Under the strain of the last months he had broken down. In his fever he seemed to hear the cries of the starving citizens. Would they give in before the ships could sail to their relief?

It was the 1st of September when the Sea Beggars embarked in their shallow boats on the water that was now slowly rising over the land. The little fleet made its way over fifteen miles of flooded country between the sea-coast and Leyden. So far a favourable wind had blown them onwards. Now the wind changed, the waters began to sink, and despair once more fell on the starving people within Leyden. They had eaten everything now. They had boiled the leaves of trees and eaten roots. Women and children dropped down dead in the streets, the burghers could hardly drag their weary legs up to the watch-tower. Yet they would not give up. "Leyden was sublime in her despair." They must be true to their charge, true to their Prince, true to their country. The old burgomaster of the town spoke to the wavering from time to time.

"My life is at your disposal," he said one day. "Here is my sword. Plunge it into me and divide my flesh among you. But expect no surrender as long as I live."

"As well," shouted the angry Spaniards—"As well can the Prince of Orange pluck the stars from the sky as bring the ocean to the walls of Leyden."

On the 1st of October a violent gale swept over
the waste of waters from the north-west. The
waters rose rapidly, and the Sea Beggars sailed
proudly forward in the darkness of the night.

Within the town all was mysterious. Would
the Spaniards attack them or flee? Must they yet
perish in sight of help?

But before morning had dawned the Spanish
host had grown alarmed at the rapidly rising waters,
and the crews of wild fierce sailors sailing ever
nearer and nearer. And before the waters reached
them they had crept away under cover of the
darkness.

A long line of moving lights were seen to flit
across the black face of the waters at dead of night,
and when day dawned at last there was not a
Spaniard left. Only a boy stood waving his cap
from the summit of the Spanish fort, a boy who
had seen the enemy's flight and had had the
courage to go and wave the signal. So the Sea
Beggars sailed to Leyden and the city was saved.

The Prince of Orange had a new and beautiful
town built up to celebrate the victory over Spain.
And as long as the world rolls on, this splendid
story of heroic defence will be told and retold with
ever-growing enthusiasm.

13. WILLIAM THE SILENT.

"As long as he lived he was the guiding star of a whole brave nation, and when he died the little children cried in the streets."   —MOTLEY.

WILLIAM THE SILENT now became more popular than ever. Untiring was his work for his country's good, unwearying his patience, unflagging his energy. But he saw more plainly than ever that the Netherlands, now split up into seventeen provinces, must be united in the face of a common foe, and to this end he worked.

"Union is important above all," he cried to his chosen people. "Act together. Separate twigs can be snapped in two easily, but no one is strong enough to break a fagot. Unite yourselves firmly. Do this and the people will be a shield and buckler of their rights, and will no longer ebb and flow like the waves of the sea. Do this and you will be an example to all free people and to all unjust oppressors."

A terrible massacre of Protestants at Antwerp soon showed how right he was in his advice. The Spaniard was yet bent on the destruction of those who had accepted the Reformed faith, and this terrible deed, known to history as the "Spanish Fury," by which 8000 people lost their lives, showed that something must be done and at once.

In 1577 a union was decided on at Ghent between the seventeen provinces, and it is known
as the Pacification of Ghent.   There is a curious
old Dutch picture representing the seventeen provinces as seventeen ladies, each holding the coat
of arms of a province.   They are all penned like
sheep in an enclosure, the entrance of which is
guarded by the Belgian lion with shield and sword.
All around the peaceful enclosure stand men at
arms with guns and bayonets, while three great
cannons stand facing the entrance.   It is typical
of the strength of the union.

But the troubles of the Netherlands were not
over yet.   Spain now sent one of her strongest and
best generals to try and quell the disturbances.

Don John of Austria was half-brother of Philip,
King of Spain, and son of the late Emperor Charles
V.   He had already done much for Spain, and was
known as the "hero of Lepanto" for a famous
victory that he had gained.   He now entered
Brussels with a flourish of trumpets as Governor-
General of the country.

Meanwhile, at the request of his people, William
the Silent made a tour of the newly united provinces.   His reception was simple and pathetic.
There were no triumphal arches, no martial music,
only the cries wrung from the hearts of the people,
" Father William is come ! Father William is come !"
He had guided them through the storm.   He would
deliver them yet.

But even the Prince could not do the impossible. Don John with a large Spanish army came against him and defeated the Netherlanders near Brussels. Further union was now necessary, and in the year 1579 the famous "Union of Utrecht" was made, strengthening the union at Ghent and laying the foundation of the powerful Republic of the United Netherlands, which was to play its part in the world's history.

Out of chaos and night a new light seemed dawning—but slowly.

It was recognised that the Prince was a danger, and that he must be got rid of somehow. A price was accordingly set upon his head. It was March 15, 1580, when the famous ban was put forth by Spain declaring William of Orange to be a traitor to his country, and ordering that he be banished from the realm. He, who had already beggared himself to serve his country, was now to be an outlaw, an exile, a traitor. He answered the ban by the ever-famous document known as his "Apology."

"I am in the hand of God," he pleaded; "my worldly goods and my life have long been given to His service."

So much did he love his country, that he was willing to go into exile if his absence would help them.

"What reward can I hope after my long service and the almost total wreck of my earthly fortunes,

if not the prize of having acquired your liberty?"
he cried to his people. "If then, my masters, you
judge that my absence or my death can serve you,
behold me ready to obey. Command me—send
me to the ends of the earth—I will go. But, if
you judge that my life can yet be of service to
you, I dedicate it afresh to you and to the
country."

This was followed by a further step in the
direction of liberty. The men of the Netherlands
drew up a Declaration of Independence refusing
any longer to be subject to Spain. William of
Orange was their Prince and master—him only
would they obey.

But William their Prince was not to be with
them much longer. A price was already on his
head. As he had lived for them, so now he was
to die for them. The summer of 1584 found him
living at Delft, a quiet little old-world city near
Rotterdam. It was a Sunday morning when a
shabby, travel-stained man begged for money
wherewith to buy some shoes and stockings to
attend church. The Prince, on hearing this,
ordered a sum of money to be given him. Next
day the poor man, whose name was Gerard, bought
a pair of pistols with the Prince's own money. The
following day the Prince with his wife on his arm
went into the dining-room about midday. He rose
to leave for his own room, when suddenly a man
emerged from a dark corner and shot him. As he

felt what had happened, the Prince fell back into the arms of one of his servants.

"O God, have mercy upon this poor people!" he uttered with touching pathos.

They were his last words. A few minutes later he breathed his last. Bitterly the country mourned him. "Father William" was gone from them. He had borne the load of the people's sorrows, their name had been the last word on his lips. True, indeed, were the last words of the historian who so loved him: "As long as he lived he was the guiding star of a whole brave nation, and when he died the little children cried in the street."

Ever grateful have the Dutch people been to the House of Orange. Still the colours of William the Silent are their colours; still his motto, "I will maintain," is their national motto; still one of the House of Orange rules the country. And when Dutchmen have left their shores and gone to dwell in distant lands beyond the sea, still the name of Orange has marked their love of this ancient hero, and the Orange River Colony in South Africa, no less than the Orange county in New York State, America, bear testimony that William the Silent has never been forgotten.

14. ENGLAND.

"This happy breed of men, this little world,
This precious stone set in the silver sea."
—SHAKSPERE.

UP to this time Spain had been the strongest and mightiest nation in Europe. Not only did she rule a great part of Italy, Sicily, the Netherlands, nearly all North America, all South America, but Portugal had fallen to her, with rich possessions in South Africa and India.

She commanded the land, because she commanded the sea. Her galleys were in every port and harbour of the known world, trading with all the rich countries under her sway.

It has been truly said, "Whosoever commands the sea, commands the trade: whosoever commands the trade of the world, commands the riches of the world, and consequently the world itself."

This, then, was quite true of Spain in the sixteenth century. She was the first empire in the world of whom it could be said that the sun never set on her dominions. This sunny Spain, washed by the waters of the great Atlantic on one side and the blue Mediterranean on the other, was yet looking round for new worlds to conquer when as yet the other nations of Europe had scarce ventured beyond their own fishing-grounds. The largest merchant ship of either England or Holland was not fit to brave the storms of the Atlantic. But the sea - loving spirit of the old Vikings was in these northern countries. It had slept through the long ages of over five hundred years, but now it was to burst forth again with its old vigour and its old strength. England and Holland were side by side to regain the mastery of wind and wave, until Spain lay crushed and powerless before their superior seamanship.

How did it all come about? What was this race of English who manned the ships that carried the flag of their country round the world, who fought the Spaniard on his own ground, who destroyed his "invincible" fleet, known to history as the Spanish Armada?

How did this little island, "set in a silver sea," manage to destroy the great power of Spain, and finally possess themselves of an empire on which the sun never sets?

The answer lies in the romantic life - story of the old sea-captain Drake, and the encouragement given to sailors by the English queen under whom he sailed, the "Good Queen Bess" of the sixteenth century.

But before beginning this old story it will be well to see what had been happening in England while Spain was so busy trying to crush out the Protestants in the Netherlands. What part had

this England played in the great Awakening of
mankind, and in the Reformation that had spread
over Europe ?

England has been called the " sea-cradle of the
Reformation," because it was by reason of the
Reformation that the King of England, Henry
VIII., was induced to strengthen his coasts and
build his navy to protect Protestant England
against Roman Catholic Spain.   Like the Netherlands, England had taken a strong Protestant line ;
when the choice had to be made, Henry VIII. had
cast off the supreme power of the Pope but retained
the title of " Defender of the Faith," a title which
to this day is borne by sovereigns of England.

There was danger in the air.   The whole country
was divided into two sides.   France became Roman
Catholic and sided with Spain.   England must prepare for possible invasion.

Now, when Henry VIII. came to the throne
England had no fleet at all.   A few merchant
hulks traded with Lisbon and Antwerp, a fishing
fleet sailed to Iceland for cod.   It is true that
Cabot had sailed across the Atlantic,[1] but his
enterprise had not been followed up, and Spain
ruled the waters as before.

But Henry VIII. was not blind to the needs of
the nation.   If war broke out, the merchant and
fishing ships must help to defend the coast.   He
repaired all the important dockyards and built

[1] See Book II. chapter 41.

fortresses, ruins of which may still be seen from
Berwick to the Land's End. He built new ships
capable of carrying guns. The Great Harry was
the wonder of the day; she carried 700 men and
was 1000 tons burden. But when Henry died the
fleet perished. His daughter Mary was a stern
Roman Catholic, and, married to Philip of Spain,
there was no further danger of war with that
great empire. The new queen was too busy
warring against Protestantism to look to the seas;
her father's fine ships rotted in the harbours.
She left the seas to privateers — that is, to any
men who were rich enough to buy, fit out, and
command ships for themselves.

And this privateering ruled the day till the
death of Mary in 1558, when her sister Elizabeth
came to the throne. Elizabeth was an English
woman; she loved the spirit of adventure and
enterprise that took her sailor subjects on the
high seas. She encouraged privateering, for the
risk was small and the hope of profit was great.
So she became the restorer of England's naval
glory, the "Queen of the Northern Seas."

15. ELIZABETH'S SAILORS.

"Brave the captain was ; the seamen
     Made a gallant crew,
Gallant sons of English freedom,
     Sailors bold and true."
                                    —TENNYSON.

Now, of all the great sailors who helped Queen
Elizabeth to build up England's sea power, the
greatest was Francis Drake. Of all the heroes
whose exploits have set our world's history aglow
with romance, there is not one more thrilling than
the life-story of this man. His every deed from
the cradle to the grave is a story. The first sight
of him is as a small blue-eyed, curly-haired boy in
the midst of a party of desperate Protestants in
Devonshire flying for their lives from an outburst
of Roman Catholic fury. Coming of a large Protestant family, the boy grew up full of hatred for
the Church of Rome.

At the time of the abdication of Charles V. he
was fifteen, and already apprenticed to the master
of a small ship plying between England and the
Netherlands. There he would hear of Philip's
tyranny, of Alva's massacres, of the Netherlands
revolt.

His rough school on the high seas was not
without its reward. He became a remarkably
clever sailor, and when the skipper of his ship died
he left it to young Francis Drake.

"But the narrow seas were a prison for so large
a spirit born for greater undertakings," and the
very year that the Counts Egmont and Horn were
beheaded in Brussels, 1567, Drake was command-
ing a small ship, the Judith, in an expedition
commanded by his kinsman, John Hawkins.

Now, John Hawkins was a Devonshire man too,
and related to the Drakes. His father had been
a sailor in the time of Henry V., and his son John,
who was to do so much for the navy of England,
was about thirty at the time when Elizabeth became queen. With young Drake in command of
the Judith, and some other ships, Hawkins set sail
from Plymouth in October 1567.

The little fleet was a good deal knocked about in
the rough gales then blowing in the Bay of Biscay,
but they reached the Canary Isles in safety, and
sailed thence to some of the Spanish settlements
along the coast of America. Here, having collected
a vast store of gold, silver, and jewels, they turned
homewards. But a gale blew them into the Gulf
of Mexico, where they knew full well no welcome
would await them from the Spaniards there. How-
ever, they made a treaty and stopped to repair
their injured ships. But treachery was in the air,
and without note or warning the Spaniards suddenly attacked them furiously. Bravely enough
they tried to defend their ships and their cargo,
but at last they had to escape as best they might,
Hawkins in one battered ship and Drake in another.

On the 23rd of January 1569 a weather-beaten
man was riding post - haste from Plymouth to
London with tidings of a desperate fray with the
Spaniards.   It was Francis Drake, and soon all
England was ringing with the news, which had
the great result that trade between Spain and
England was stopped.   It was the beginning of
the end.

True, Hawkins and Drake became the heroes of
the hour ; but over England herself a fierce war-
cloud lowered, the horizon was dark with the
danger of coming storm.   The Netherlands were
in open revolt against Spain, but so far England
had taken no part publicly.

The very year that the Beggars of the Sea were
sailing to Brille, Drake was stealing secretly away
from Plymouth port with a little fleet and crew of
seventy-three men, all under the age of thirty, on
a desperate venture against Spain on the farther
side of the Atlantic.   He had found out that
Philip's treasure from the mines of Peru was
landed at Panama, and carried across the narrow
neck of land on the backs of many mules, to be
re-shipped for Spain on the other side.

"I have brought you to the treasure-house of
the world," cried Drake, when he had sailed
safely across the broad Atlantic.   "Blame yourselves if you go away empty."

They were but a handful of men against the
Spaniards, who attacked them.   As Drake led his

little party of adventurers forward he was badly wounded, and fainted from loss of blood. This prevented the Spanish treasure from being carried off by the English. The sun rose next morning on their glorious failure, and the famous attempt on the " treasure-house of the world" was at an end.

But Drake was still undaunted. Disasters befell him. His brother died in his arms, thirty of his little band died of sickness, others were too ill to stand. It is impossible to follow all his adventures, but the story of how he first saw the Pacific Ocean must be told. With eighteen men and native guides he started off to climb the forest-clad spurs of the dividing ridge of mountains dividing the two seas. The expedition was not unlike that of Balboa some sixty years before.[1] Arrived at the top, he climbed a tree, and for the first time an Englishman gazed on the vast Southern Sea, named by Magellan the Pacific Ocean. Returning to his men, he fell on his knees, like a crusader of old, and besought " Almighty God of His goodness to give him life and leave to sail once in an English ship on that sea."

It was a great moment in the history of England. Jealously had Spain guarded this Southern Sea which now lay under the eyes of an Englishman.

[1] See Book II. chapter 42.

16. DRAKE'S VOYAGE ROUND THE WORLD.

"Coastwise—cross seas—round the world and back again."
                              —KIPLING.

DRAKE'S chance came at last, and with the sanction
of his queen he sailed out of Plymouth harbour,
bound for the chartless ocean, hitherto only crossed
by Magellan.

It was the middle of November in the year 1577.
Drake was now thirty-two, in the prime of his
strength and manhood. Dressed in his seaman's
shirt, belted at the waist, a scarlet cap with gold
band on his head, he waved his farewell to England
from the deck of his flagship the Pelican, a small
vessel indeed for the vast expedition before him.
The seamen—some 150 in number—knew nothing
of their destination, but they must have guessed,
from the twenty guns on the Pelican, that there
was danger ahead.

There was, indeed, danger ahead, but there was
danger on board too. Second in command of the
little fleet was one Thomas Doughty. His conduct
was suspicious from the very first, and by the time
South America was reached there was no longer
any room to doubt that he was a traitor. Having
run the ships into a harbour on the coast of Pata-
gonia, Drake called his men together to take council
what should be done. It was the spot where

Magellan had tried his mutinous men years ago,
and the stump of his gallows stood on the desolate
wind-swept shore. The trial lasted two days.
The case was even more desperate than Drake
had imagined. Doughty had betrayed the queen's
secret, he had nearly upset the whole expedition.

"They that think this man worthy of death, let
them, with me, hold up their hands," cried Drake at
the last.

As the words left his lips a throng of brown
hands were raised. The traitor must die. A block
was prepared. An altar was raised beside it. Then
the two old friends, Drake and Doughty, knelt side
by side to ask forgiveness; rising, they kissed one
another, and in another minute the sword had
fallen, and as Doughty's head was held up to view,
Drake cried, "Lo, this is the end of traitors."

From this moment his rule was undisputed.
Treason and mutiny played no further part in the
expedition. Boldly now Drake entered the Straits
of Magellan, bound for the Southern Sea. Storms
and tempests burst upon the little ships, but
the commander's splendid seamanship triumphed
over unknown dangers, till after fourteen days
they sailed out into the Pacific Ocean. Here a
terrific storm burst upon them. The sky was
dark, by night and day the wind roared and
howled. This went on for fifty-three days, at the
end of which time Drake found himself alone.
His little fleet had entirely disappeared. But the

winds had driven him farther south than any ship had been before. He landed on an unknown island, and laying himself flat on the earth, he embraced with his arms the southernmost point of the world, now known as Cape Horn.

A month later a Spanish ship was lazily waiting in the harbour of Valparaiso for a wind to carry her to Panama with a cargo of gold from Peru, when a sail hove in sight. The Spaniards ran up flags and beat their drums to welcome their supposed countrymen. The Pelican shot alongside and English sailors leapt on board, crying, " Down, dogs ! down !" as they caught and bound the astonished Spaniards. It was not long before the Spanish crew were stowed safely away, and their precious cargo was transferred to the Pelican. For three days the plunder went on. The English, who had lived on salt penguin for months, were refreshed, and the Pelican, richly freighted with Spanish goods, sailed northwards with its prize.

Still chasing and plundering Spanish ships on the coast of South America, Drake made his way northwards and ever northwards, up the coast of North America to San Francisco, still hugging his treasure. The cold was intense, his rigging was frozen, his crew sick, but his hot courage never failed him.

On July 25, 1579, he struck across the unknown ocean, bound for the Moluccas. As if by inspiration, he pushed on and on. Sixty-eight days passed with no signs of land, till at last he reached the Philippine Islands, where Magellan had met his tragic end.

It would take too long to tell of the homeward voyage, by the Cape of Good Hope, — how the treasure-laden ship ran on to a reef among the East India Islands, and how even her commander gave her up as lost; but she overcame all difficulties and accomplished her great exploit. It was three years after Drake had sailed from England that the Pelican, whose name was now changed to the Golden Hind, laboured into Plymouth Sound. The prayer uttered by Drake six years before had been fulfilled. He had sailed the Pacific Ocean in an English ship, and he had sailed it from side to side. Its secret was England's at last, and, laden with its wealth, the triumphant explorer was now stepping ashore to lay his booty at the feet of his queen.

Soon all England was ringing with his name. Elizabeth herself went to Plymouth, and, after a banquet on board, knighted the "master thief of the unknown world." She ordered the Golden Hind to be preserved for ever as a worthy rival of Magellan's Victoria.

The tide of the great Spanish empire had turned at last.

17. THE GREAT ARMADA.

"When that great fleet Invincible against her bore in vain
The richest spoils of Mexico, the stoutest hearts of Spain."
—MACAULAY.

THE romantic daring of Drakes voyage and the vastness of his spoil roused great enthusiasm in England. But the honours heaped upon him by Elizabeth were looked on by Philip of Spain with fierce anger. She had accepted his stolen treasure, and plans with regard to the conquest of England now began to take shape. The dockyards of Spain became busy centres, and the first ships of that great Armada, or armed force, destined for war with England, began to collect in the Tagus. If England were conquered, the empire of Spain would be safe, so thought Philip, whose possessions even now rivalled the Roman empire of old.

That a great fleet was building in Spain soon became known in England, and Drake hurried off to the scene of action. He sailed to Cadiz, entered the harbour, sank the guardship, sent flying a fleet of ships intended for the invasion of England, set fire to others, and sailed out again, having lost neither man nor boat.

"I have singed the King of Spain's beard this time," said Drake, while all Europe was wondering at his last adventure.

Then, not content with having delayed the

Armada, he seized the largest Spanish merchant ship afloat, laden with spoil from India, which he towed triumphantly into Dartmouth harbour. Not only was it the richest cargo that had ever entered an English port, but on board were found papers telling of the richness and mysteries of the East Indian trade, hitherto known only to Spain and Portugal.

By the end of April 1588 the Spanish Armada was ready.

July found the fleet—named by the Spaniards the Invincible Armada — at the mouth of the English Channel with a fair wind. It was formidable enough as it sailed on in the form of a crescent extending for seven miles. There were 130 ships, standing high out of the water. On board were guns, many soldiers and sailors, priests, surgeons, and food for six months. The whole was under the command of the Duke of Medina Sidonia, from whose flagship waved the Imperial banner, bearing on one side the crucified Christ and on the other His mother Mary; for this was not only an attack on England, it was an attack on England's Protestantism too.

It was the 19th of July when the Spanish fleet, so long expected, was seen by the English off the coast of Cornwall. At once fires of alarm were lit along the coast.

"Far on the deep the Spaniards saw, along each southern shire,
    Cape beyond cape, in endless range, those twinkling points of
        fire."

Playing bowls with his Captains.

When the news arrived at Plymouth, the English commander, Lord Howard of Effingham, was playing bowls with his captains. None knew better than Drake what the news meant. There was not a moment to lose, for the English ships were all huddled in ports along the coast at the mercy of the Spanish. On the other hand, a panic would spoil all. He refused to stop playing bowls.

"There is time to play the game and beat the Spaniards," he said quietly.

But there was no sleep for England that night. While in port and harbour the ships were manned and sailed, bells of alarm rang out all night, horsemen gathered together, cannon's roar and notes of the bugle broke the silence of the night.

"Night sank upon the dusky beach and on the purple sea,
    Such night in England ne'er had been, nor e'er again shall be."

There was but one hope for the English in this desperate struggle. Her ships, though fewer, were lighter and faster-sailing than those of the enemy, therefore a close encounter would be fatal. Worrying and harrying the Spanish fleet, the English ships pursued them up the English Channel till Calais was reached. For nearly a week this running fight had lasted. By July 29 the Spaniards had lost 4000 men : three great ships had sunk ; their masts were shot away, the men had lost heart. The Spanish commander decided to retreat to Spain by way of Scotland.

Nevertheless, as Drake said, the fleet seemed still "wonderful great and strong." The "work of destruction was reserved for a mightier foe than Drake." Suddenly the wind rose into a storm, which drove pursuers and pursued across to the Netherlands. Narrowly escaping shipwreck on the flat coast of Holland, the shattered Armada was driven pitilessly northwards, hurrying before the wind.

"There was never anything pleased me better," said Drake as he followed after, "than seeing the enemy flying with a southerly wind to the northwards."

Supplies fell short and forced the English ships to give up the chase. The Spaniards sailed on to the Orkney Islands at the north of Scotland, where the storms of the northern seas broke on them furiously. Round the coast they staggered, scattering the shores with their wrecks. Eight thousand Spaniards perished near the Giant's Causeway; 1100 bodies were washed up on to the coast of Ireland. Out of the magnificent fleet that had sailed from Spain only fifty ships returned, bearing a few thousand sick and maimed Spaniards.

"I sent you to fight against men and not with the winds," said Philip to his unfortunate commander, who slunk away to his home to be tormented ever after by boys crying under his window, "Drake is coming! Drake is coming!"

It was indeed Drake's name with which Europe
rang as the news of the victory spread, though
Elizabeth acknowledged the power of the storm
when she struck a medal with this motto, "God
blew with His wind and they were scattered."

18. AMONG THE ICEBERGS.

"And now there came both mist and snow,
    And it grew wondrous cold."
                                    —COLERIDGE.

BESIDES Howard, Drake, and Hawkins, no one
had been of more use in pursuing the Spanish
Armada than Martin Frobisher.

Born in 1535, he had been at sea all his life;
for he was one of the first among early explorers
to sail amid the ice of the far north in search
of a passage to China by North America. For
years past it had been the dream of every voy-
ager to find a short way to the East by which
English wares could be exchanged for the pearls
and spice of India without the long voyage by
the Cape of Good Hope.

It had been the dream of Cabot, and the dream
of Sir Hugh Willoughby, who had perished in the
attempt. It was now the dream of Martin Frobisher. The discovery of the north-west passage,
he said, was "the only thing of the world that
was yet left undone by which a notable mind

might be made famous and fortunate." He did not care for plundering Spanish ships laden with treasure. Rather did he look for honour for his country, fame for himself, knowledge of new lands for the whole world. The idea did not appeal to his countrymen, and, like Columbus [1] before him, he asked for ships and money in vain.

For thirteen long years he toiled, until at last a patron arose to supply the necessary funds, and in the year 1576 two little ships, the Gabriel and Michael, left England for the ice-bound regions of the north. Wondrous, indeed, was the courage of the man who set forth on such an expedition of danger, with two small ships and a crew of only thirty-five men.

Queen Elizabeth stood at an open window of her palace at Greenwich waving farewell to the captain of this little fleet bound for unknown seas of ice. She recognised the greatness of his spirit and the daring of his adventure, but she had not stirred a finger to get him new ships for his perilous undertaking.

So Frobisher sailed away to the north by the eastern coast of England and the north of Scotland. Here a furious storm broke over the little ships, and before ever Frobisher had reached the icy coast of Greenland the Gabriel was alone. The Michael had deserted and gone home with the story that Frobisher himself had perished in a storm. Mean-

[1] Book II. chapter 35.

while the captain was sailing bravely onwards with
his storm-shattered ship and his diminished crew of
eighteen.

"I will sacrifice my life to God rather than
return home without discovering a north - west
passage to Cathay," he said to his men with that
enthusiasm which alone can carry a man through
great enterprises. And the men, catching his
spirit of courage, sailed their battered ship across
to the shores of Labrador. Amid a group of
American islands he entered what seemed to be
a strait that might lead to the East. Bearing in
mind Magellan's Straits, leading from the Atlantic
to the Pacific by South America, he named these
Frobisher's Straits, hoping they might lead from
ocean to ocean by North America. Further than
all former mariners he sailed into this unknown
sea. Yet for all his courage, the expedition failed :
man after man died, the weather grew very cold,
snow fell heavily, and reluctantly he sailed home.

A curious thing now happened. A stone which
he had brought from the frozen regions to England was said to contain gold. Martin Frobisher
sprang into fame. A new fleet was at once fitted
out, not for the discovery of the north-west passage,
but for the discovery of more gold. The queen
sent a large ship of her own this time ; men offered
their services by the score ; Frobisher was made
High Admiral of all seas and waters, countries,
lands, and isles, of the icy north, and in 1577 he

sailed off on his second expedition. The fleet did
not go far, but it returned laden with supposed
gold. Kneeling on the frozen snow, the little party
of Englishmen had taken possession of the country
in the name of the queen, leaving a cross of stones
and the English flag flying.

While Drake was sailing round the world, Martin
Frobisher was being given command of a yet more
famous fleet of fifteen ships, so that he should sail
to the frozen land of gold, and leave there a little
colony of Englishmen to protect English interests
from strangers. Away sailed the magnificent fleet,
away once more to the northern coast of America,
towards Frobisher's Straits. Amid snow and ice,
fogs and gales, the ships made their way. One
vessel was crushed between mighty icebergs. In
a thick fog the ships lost their course, but Frobisher
now made the greatest discovery of his life. He
had found out that Frobisher's Straits were no
straits, but a bay.

Now, to the north of Frobisher's Bay he was sailing west, through another channel, which might lead
on into the open sea beyond. In reality he was sailing up the straits known later as Hudson's Straits,
and he was close on the entrance to the great inland
sea of North America, when he turned back to fulfil
his orders and search for gold. The ships returned
home with their freight of stones, but by this time
England was raging with disappointment, for little
enough gold had been produced from the black

stones of the frozen north, and no more ships were sent in search of it. The plan of a colony was given up. It was three hundred years before the north-west passage into the Pacific Ocean was found,[1] after many a ship had been lost and many a life laid down. Intricate enough was the channel that led from sea to sea, and far to the north of anything that Martin Frobisher, with all his courage and with all his enthusiasm, could ever have found with the imperfect ships at his command.

19. SIR HUMPHREY GILBERT.

"He sat upon the deck,
  The Book was in his hand.
'Do not fear. Heaven is as near,'
He said, 'by water as by land.'"
—LONGFELLOW.

ELIZABETH had been Queen of England for twenty years before any steps were taken to colonise the New World, towards which all eyes were turned. But while she and her adventurers were dazzled by dreams of gold in the frozen regions of the north, one of her subjects was watching the English fishermen on the coasts of Newfoundland and planning homes for them in America.

This man was Sir Humphrey Gilbert. Year by year ships came from Spain and Portugal, England and France, to the shores of this Newfoundland, and

[1] See Book V. chapter 12.

here it was that Gilbert planned a little colony of
his own countrymen. His most faithful friend and
adviser was his step-brother, Walter Raleigh, who
was hereafter to play a large part among Elizabeth's seamen. Both were Devonshire men, like
Drake and Hawkins; but Gilbert was among the
first Englishmen to see that the love of adventure,
which was leading so many at this time to annoy
the Spaniards, might be turned to better account.
England, he thought, was playing an ignoble part.
Instead of taking the lead in voyages of discovery,
as she might have done, with the best of ships and
sailors, she had given herself up to plundering the
treasure-ships of Spain. Drake was the hero of the
hour. The queen herself had shared his ill-gotten
plunder. The cry of Elizabeth's England was for gold.

So when Gilbert undertook the task of carrying
English colonists to the shores of the New World,
Elizabeth tried to turn him from his purpose. He
was willing to brave the displeasure of his royal
mistress. There was no gold to be got out of his
lofty scheme, but he stood firm. He had dreams of
making his colony a starting-point for the north-
west passage. He was no common adventurer. He
had a great mind and a great soul.

"He is not worthy to live at all that, for fear
or danger of death, shunneth his country's service
and his own honour, seeing death is inevitable and
the fame of virtue immortal," he used to say when
pleading for the Arctic voyage.

In 1578, when Drake was sailing round the world
in his little Pelican, and Frobisher was fighting his
way amid the frozen seas of the north, Sir Humphrey Gilbert was collecting ships and men to
plant his colony over the seas. With eleven ships
and some 500 men he sailed across the Atlantic
Ocean to Newfoundland, but from the very beginning the expedition was a failure. One of the ships
was lost, and misfortune after misfortune compelled
the rest to return.

Undaunted, he tried again. With Walter
Raleigh's help he fitted out a second expedition.
In 1583 the little fleet left England with a parting
gift from the queen in the shape of a golden
anchor. But again a series of disasters overtook
the expedition. Two days after leaving harbour
the largest ship in the fleet deserted. Angrily
Gilbert sailed on without it, arriving in safety on
the shores of Newfoundland. Summoning Spanish
and Portuguese together, he raised a pillar with
the arms of England engraved on it, and formally took possession of the country in the queen's
name.

But it was not easy to keep order. The sailors,
after the manner of their day, were lawless adventurers, pirates, and robbers. They only wanted to
make their fortune; they had no industry, perseverance, or endurance—qualities needed for all
colonisation.

Everything went wrong, and at last the would-be

colonists begged to be taken home.   Only two ships were left, the Squirrel and the Golden Hind.   Gilbert commanded the Squirrel, the smallest of the two, and totally unfit to "pass through the ocean sea at that season of the year."

But "I will not forsake my little company going homeward, with whom I have passed through so many storms and perils," said their commander. The weather was very wild, the oldest sailor on board had never seen "more outrageous seas."

The Squirrel could not weather them, and one night she foundered with all hands.   Gilbert was last seen, his Bible in his hand, bidding his terrified companions be of good cheer.

"We are as near to heaven by water as by land," he cried as the little Squirrel went down into the deep Atlantic with her brave commander. Though he failed, Sir Humphrey Gilbert was called the Father of American colonisation, because it was he who first turned men's thoughts from plundering exploits to the higher aims of civilisation.

20. VIRGINIA.

"The silent ocean of the past, a waste
Of water weltering over graves."
—CULLEN BRYANT.

THOUGH Sir Humphrey Gilbert had laid down his life, his efforts at colonisation had not been in vain. His step-brother, Sir Walter Raleigh, now took up his work, in something of the same spirit, though his efforts, too, were doomed to failure.

At this time Raleigh was in high favour at the Court of Elizabeth, and she readily helped him to follow in Gilbert's steps and found a colony in America.

So on April 27, 1584, two sea-captains with their ships left England to find some suitable part of the country with good soil, good water, and possibly gold, as yet unclaimed by Spaniards. The sea-captains, following the track of Columbus, sailed to the West Indies, whence they coasted north-wards some 120 miles and entered a harbour which seemed promising. They knelt down, thanked God for their safe arrival, and took possession of the country in the name of Queen Elizabeth and her courtier Raleigh.

The beauty of the new country filled them with rapture. Wild grapes grew in plenty, the forests were filled with birds, the air was delicious, the growth luxuriant. There was no doubt this would make a grand site for the first English colony over the seas. Would the native Indians object ?

" Oh no," said the sea - captains when they arrived in England. " The natives were most gentle, loving, and faithful, void of all guile and treason, and such as lived after the manner of the Golden Age."

Raleigh listened to this glowing account and

decided to begin a colony there at once. His fame
rose higher than ever, for he had given to his queen
a new country, to which she now gave the name
of Virginia, after herself — the Virgin Queen —
while Raleigh was to become "lord and governor
of Virginia."

Seven ships and a hundred colonists were soon
ready, under the command of Sir Richard Grenville, who with Drake, Hawkins, and Frobisher
stood in the forefront of Elizabeth's sea-heroes.
After eighty days on the high seas, Grenville's
fleet arrived on the coast of Virginia. All looked
fair and prosperous.

"It is the goodliest soil under heaven — the
paradise of the world," said Sir Richard Grenville with enthusiasm, as he set to work to make
the new colony a success. But his little band of
Englishmen turned out to be gold-seekers rather
than colonists. They lived on food furnished by
the Indians, while they made search for gold, until the day came that the Indians turned on them,
fighting took place, and the supply of food was
stopped. Matters grew from bad to worse. Starvation stared them in the face. Their commander
had sailed to England for help. They were in
despair, when an English ship one day hove in
sight, with Sir Francis Drake on board bringing
aid for the colony. With one accord the would-be
colonists begged to be taken home, and Drake
could not refuse them; one and all embarked

for England, and so perished the next attempt at colonising Virginia.

An old story tells us that these colonists first brought the tobacco-plant back to England, for they had learnt to smoke from the Indians. But we know now that Hawkins had already introduced it into England years before this, and that Drake and Raleigh were both great smokers.

One day, the story runs, Raleigh sat smoking his pipe, when his servant entered his room with a flask of spiced ale. Aghast at seeing smoke coming from his master's mouth, as if he were on fire, he dashed the contents of the flask into Raleigh's face.

The first potato is said to have been planted in Ireland by Sir Walter Raleigh, though again Hawkins and Drake had been before him by introducing it into England and Germany. And a German poet, Heine, quaintly remarked, "Luther shook Germany to its foundation, but Drake pacified it again : he gave us the potato."

Yet once more Raleigh fitted out a colony for Virginia. This time seventeen women were sent to make comfortable the new homes beyond the sea. Under the command of John White they sailed away for the New World, but again they were doomed to failure. The Indians refused help and food, and fighting took place. The only brightness amid the general gloom was the birth of a child, the first English baby born in America,

called after the colony, Virginia. Matters grew
worse, and John White sailed to England for help.
He arrived to find the Spanish Armada threatening
the invasion of England ; no one had any thoughts
for the distant colony in the Far West. The Armada
came and went before anything was done, and when
White at last reached the shores of Virginia, he
found the place a desert, every trace of the colonists
gone, nor was anything ever heard of them again !

And so perished Raleigh's second attempt at
colonising in America. He fitted out no more
expeditions, and it was many years before anything further was done in this direction.

21. STORY OF THE REVENGE.

"Fall into the hands of God, not into the hands of Spain."
—TENNYSON.

THOUGH Sir Richard Grenville had not succeeded
with the first colony in Virginia, yet he was a
very able sailor, and Raleigh now sent him on an
important expedition, to lie in wait for Spanish
ships returning laden from the West Indies.

Midway between Spain and the West Indies,
in the midst of the Atlantic Ocean, is a little
group of islands called the Azores. Thither sailed
the English fleet, consisting of six battleships
only, to obey orders. The ships were lying at

anchor under one of the islands, called Flores, one summer day, when a Spanish fleet of fifty sail bore down upon them. It was certain death to fight so large a number, and there was no choice but to sail away as fast as possible and escape. The English ships were soon ready, all save one, the Revenge. She was under the command of Sir Richard Grenville.

"I have ninety sick men ashore," he said; "I cannot and will not leave them to fall into the hands of Spain."

With his own hands he helped to carry the sick men on board as fast as possible, so that he might sail away with the rest. But it took time, and the little Revenge had not sailed far when the Spanish fleet bore down. By this time the rest of the English fleet had gone and the Revenge was alone.

"We will fight our way through the Spanish fleet or we will die," cried Sir Richard; his men caught the brave enthusiasm, and steered their ship on into almost certain death.

The Spanish ships came on, sometimes five at a time, and the Spaniards boarded the little English ship, and fought her sailors hand to hand, but each time they were driven back disabled.

All through the long August night the fight continued. But each great Spanish galleon was defeated in turn, until by dawn fifteen had attacked her in vain. Some had been sunk at her side, and others were ashamed to attempt further fighting.

"And the night went down, and the sun smiled out, far over the summer sea."

"Fight on! fight on!" cried Sir Richard, though badly wounded himself and his vessel all but a wreck. "Fight on, men of Devon! fight on!"

"But as the day increased, so our men decreased," said Raleigh when he told the story afterwards.

At last forty men out of the hundred were slain, the masts of the Revenge were broken, the powder spent, and the decks strewn with wounded and dying. The Spanish ships lay round in a broken ring, watching to see what would happen next. They knew she could fight no more. Still Grenville would not surrender.

"No," he cried. "Rather will we sink the ship, that nothing of glory or victory may remain to the Spaniards. Let us fall into the hands of God, not into the hands of Spain."

The gunner was a resolute man, he was ready to do his master's bidding, but it was too much to ask of all. They had wives and children waiting for them at home.

Sir Richard now lay dying, and his seamen yielded to the Spaniards. They carried Sir Richard Grenville to the largest of the Spanish ships. If unequal to the English in fighting, the Spaniards were

at least their equal in courtesy. They bore Sir
Richard to the flagship and laid him by the mast,
while admiral and men alike praised his valour and
resolution. A few hours later, when the end was
fast approaching, Sir Richard cried : " Here die I,
Richard Grenville, with a joyful and quiet mind,
for that I have ended my life as a true soldier
ought to do, that hath fought for his country,
Queen, religion, and honour."

All England was soon ringing with this story.
Sir Richard Grenville was dead—he had lost the
fight, lost his men, lost his ship, lost his very
life ; but he had gained such glory for England,
for England's ships, for England's seamen, as the
world had never seen before. It is said that the
action of this one little English ship struck a
deeper terror into the hearts of the Spaniards than
even the destruction of the Armada herself.

" Hardly," says a modern historian, " if the most
glorious actions, which are set like jewels, in the
history of mankind, are weighed one against the
other in the balance, hardly will those 300 Spartans,[1]
who in the summer morning sat ' combing their long
hair for death ' in the passes of Thermopylæ, have
earned a more lofty estimate for themselves than
this one crew of modern Englishmen."

[1] See Book I. chapter 27.

22. SIR WALTER RALEIGH.

"God has made nobler heroes, but He never made a finer gentleman than Walter Raleigh."—R. L. STEVENSON.

RALEIGH had failed with his Virginian colony, but he still had dreams of an English colony elsewhere. The wealth that filled Spain from Mexico and Peru had filled England with envy. To gain a like rich kingdom for his queen, to extend her power and enrich her treasury,—this was Raleigh's dream. With these thoughts in his mind he turned his eyes to Guiana, a tract of country in South America of which dazzling tales had reached his ears.

Since the early days of Spanish discovery, natives had talked of a city of untold wealth—El Dorado they called it. It was richer than Peru, they said, and gold was so plentiful that the king was covered with turpentine and rolled in gold dust till he shone with the glory of gold. Expedition after expedition had left Spain for this land of wealth, but all had failed to penetrate the country. No one had yet discovered the fabulous city of El Dorado, though all would journey thither if they could.

It was early in the year 1595 that Sir Walter Raleigh left England with five ships for this much desired land of Guiana. Forty-six days later he reached the island of Trinidad—the Port of Spain,

as it was called—where he was kindly received
by the Spaniards. The early summer found the
explorers at the mouth of the river Orinoco, by
which they intended to row into the interior of
the country. Fortunately for them, they fell in
with a canoe of Indians. Raleigh in his eight-
oared boat gave chase and soon made friends with
them, taking on board the faithful pilot Ferdi-
nando to guide them up the fast-flowing river
into the unknown.

"But for this," said Raleigh afterwards, "I
think we had never found the way either to
Guiana or back to the ships."

Up the Orinoco mile after mile they rowed, but
they seemed to get no nearer to El Dorado. Twice
they were nearly wrecked, and they were beginning to despair, when suddenly the scenery changed
as if by magic. The high banks gave way to low-
lying plains, soft green grass grew close to the
water's edge, and deer came down to feed. Still
the strong current continued. Each man had
borne his full share of rowing, but the effort of
pulling everlastingly against such violence was
telling on the staunchest among them. They were
now some 400 miles from their ships, when, to add
to their troubles, a sudden and furious rising of
the river took place.

"Whosoever," says Raleigh, "had seen or proved
the fury of that river after it began to rise, would
perchance have turned his back somewhat sooner

than we did, if all the mountains had been gold or precious stones."

Having discovered a good deal about the country from natives, Raleigh turned for home. Wind and stream were with them now, bearing them down with almost alarming rapidity. One day they covered 100 miles. Raleigh had not found El Dorado, but he returned home enormously impressed with the new country.

" Guiana is a country that hath yet her maidenhood," he told the queen. " The face of the earth hath not been torn, the graves have not been opened for gold. It hath never been entered by any army of strength, never conquered by any Christian prince. Men shall find here more rich and beautiful cities, more temples adorned with gold, than either Cortes found in Mexico[1] or Pizarro in Peru, and the shining glory of this conquest will eclipse all those of the Spanish nation."

But this enthusiasm failed to inspire others in England. The queen was growing old, and it was to be many a long year before Raleigh's work was to tell.

Twenty-two years passed by and Raleigh never forgot the glories of Guiana. Elizabeth was dead, and her successor, James, had thrown Raleigh into the Tower of London, where he wrote the beginning of his ' History of the World ' and dreamed his hopeless dreams of colonisation.

[1] See Book II. chapter 48.

At last he persuaded James to let him go once more to Guiana, where he suggested he could find a gold mine to enrich the English Treasury. The rest of the story is sad enough. Storms, desertion, disease, and death followed him from the very first, and ere the expedition had reached the mouth of the Orinoco Raleigh himself was stricken down and unable to go farther. He sent on his young son, Walter—the "little Wat" of happier days gone by—with a party of men to find the mine, but fighting took place. The wrath of the Spaniards had been roused, young Raleigh was killed, and the Englishmen never reached the gold mine. Sadly Raleigh sailed home to England in his little ship the Destiny. For rousing the Spaniards, with whom England was now at peace, he was seized and condemned to die.

With the same courtly grace which he had borne through life he bade farewell to the friends who stood round. With the "dignity of a philosopher, the courage of a soldier, the faith of a Christian," he met his death.

"We have not such another head to be cut off," said one who stood by.

Raleigh had failed at the end and died a broken-hearted adventurer; but his love and faith in the future of England, as the mother of distant empires and the mistress of the seas, have won for him an undying name amid the annals of the world.

23. THE FAIRY QUEEN.

> " O, wonder
> How many goodly creatures are there here !
> How beauteous mankind is ! O brave new world
> That hath such people in't."
>   —SHAKSPERE.

WHEN Sir Walter Raleigh had done chasing the Spanish Armada from Plymouth to the North Sea, he crossed over to Ireland, where he visited his friend Edmund Spenser. That Spenser was a poet of no mean order Raleigh well knew, but he was hardly prepared for the wonderful new poem that Spenser read to him on this visit, under the name of the " Fairy Queen."

Here indeed was a poet — the first singer of Elizabeth's newly awakened England—the pioneer of that new glory which burst forth in this marvellous sixteenth century. Elizabeth must hear the poem from the poet's own lips. Together the two men made their way to England and stood before their queen. She listened with rapture. In the " Fairy Queen " she recognised herself. But the new poem was not for her alone. It was published in 1590, to be received by a burst of welcome, for did it not express the very life of the times ? It was the truest picture of the world of mystery and wonder, which was opening before the eyes of Englishmen—a mixture of the chivalry of the

middle ages and the new learning which had spread
from Italy. Here is one of the stories from the
" Fairy Queen."

In the far-off kingdom of Fairyland stood a
splendid city surrounded by a golden wall. Here
lived Gloriana the Queen of the Fairies, and to her
came all noble knights in search of adventure and
all persons in distress.

One day there arrived a royal maiden named Una,
who had journeyed from the Euphrates, away in the
Far East. She had been driven from home by a
huge and cruel dragon, which had laid waste the
country, the king and queen had fled for safety to a
strong castle, and she had come to the Fairy Queen
for help. Many a knight had tried to slay the
monster in vain. It was not long before a young
noble, known as the Red Cross Knight, at the palace
of Gloriana, undertook to go and slay the dragon, if
Una would show him the way. Away they started
together, the knight on a fiery steed, Una at his side
on a snow-white ass. Soon a storm drove them to
shelter in a deep wood, where presently they lost
their way. Finding a cave, the young knight dis-
mounted, and in spite of Una's remonstrances he
looked into a dark hole. By the light of his
glittering armour he saw an ugly monster, named
Error, lying in the cave. After a tremendous
struggle he killed the monster and returned to
Una.

" Fair knight, ye have won glory this day," she

said. "May all your adventures succeed as well as this."

On they went again. But before long the Red Cross Knight was led astray by a false lady, Duessa. Left alone and solitary, Una wandered through desert and wilderness to find her lost knight. She was lying at rest on the grass when suddenly a ramping lion rushed out of a wood. With open mouth he rushed at her greedily; but when he saw her nearer he stopped, and, instead of devouring her, he kissed her weary feet and licked her white hands. When she rose to go the lion followed her as her faithful guide.

Still searching for her Red Cross Knight, Una met Prince Arthur, the champion knight of Fairyland. His armour glittered like the rays of the sun, his tunic shone like twinkling stars with precious stones. His helmet was of gold, with a golden dragon. Ever bent on deeds of kindness, Arthur undertook to find for Una her Red Cross Knight, who was even now languishing in a dark dungeon in the castle of a giant, where dwelt the false Duessa. Horrible to behold was the monster giant who came forth to meet Arthur; but it was not long before he lay at Arthur's feet —dead. Then Arthur brought the poor Red Cross Knight, ill and low and weak. Duessa had fled, so they stayed and refreshed themselves at the castle. Then they parted from Arthur, and the

knight and his dear Una went on their way. And
at last they arrived at Una's home.

"This is the city of the great king, where eternal
peace and happiness dwell," said an old man, who
took the knight to a high mountain from whence
he could see the goodly city. "The way to it,
after long labour, will bring you to joyous rest
and endless bliss. And thou, fair knight, dost well
to succour this desolate princess till thou hast rid
her of her foe. That done, thou mayest travel this
path, which shall lead thee to the great city. And
there in after-times shalt thou be a saint and
befriend thine own nation. St George of merry
England shalt thou be."

His eyes were yet dazzled with the brightness
of the distant city when a hideous roaring sound
was heard that seemed to shake the very earth.
It came from a dreadful dragon stretched on the
sunny side of a hill. He was covered with huge
brazen scales, which he clashed together with a
dreadful noise; his huge tail was wrapped in a
hundred folds; his jaws opened like an abyss,
showing long ranges of iron teeth; his eyes blazed
like fire.

Putting Una into a place of safety, the Red
Cross Knight advanced fearlessly to his great task.
For two days and nights he fought the mighty
beast, and at the last he slew it. It was safe now
for the king and queen to appear, for the dragon
was slain. And clad in sombre robes they came

forth, old and hoary with time, to embrace their daughter Una and to give her in marriage to the conqueror of the dragon, the Red Cross Knight, St George of England.

The " Fairy Queen" was the first ideal poem that England produced, the source of her modern poetry. It lifted its readers at once into a clear, pure air. " No man can read the 'Fairy Queen' and be anything but the better for it," says a great American writer. " The land of Spenser is the land of Dreams, but it is also the land of Rest."

> " Here may thy storm-beat vessel safely ride;
> This is the port of rest from troublous toil.
> The world's sweet inn from pain and wearisome turmoil."

24. A GREAT DRAMATIST.

> " Thou who didst the stars and sunbeams know,
> Self-schooled, self-scanned, self-honoured, self-secure,
> Didst tread on earth unguessed at."
>
> —M. ARNOLD.

OF all the great men who added to the glory of Elizabeth's England, William Shakspere was the greatest, though neither the queen nor her people realised how great. Of the man himself the world knows nothing; with his work the Old and New Worlds ring even to-day. Just a poor lad, born of farmer parents at Stratford-on-Avon, he made his way to London as an actor and play-writer, and though he became popular, yet no one knew how great he really was till long years after he had died.

Now we know that he was one of the great "world-voices," "far-seeing as the sun," "the upper light of the world,"—one of the greatest men that the world has ever seen.

He had little enough book-learning, "small Latin and less Greek"; but he knew mankind, he understood human nature, as rare a gift then as it is now. And by this great gift he could make the people of Elizabeth's days laugh and cry at will. Men cared about human life : he showed them human life, showed them men and women as they really are, with all their smiles and all their sorrows, all their actions and all their thoughts. From

> " The whining schoolboy, with his satchel
> And shining morning face, creeping like snail
> Unwillingly to school."

The lonely exile crying to his king—

> " Your will be done : this must my comfort be,
> The sun that warms you here shall shine on me."

He tells his hearers of warriors and generals, of kings and statesmen,

> "Of old, unhappy, far-off things,
> And battles long ago."

There is a whole play about Julius Cæsar[1] and another about Coriolanus.[2] Like Spenser, too, this poet can take us into the fairy world. His fairy

---

[1] See Book I. chapter 50.   [2] See Book I. chapter 36.

queen is called Titania, and the kingdom of the
fairies is away in the Indies, where the fairy Puck
and his comrades circle the earth. These fairies
have all the secrets of nature : they dance in the
moonbeams, and they sleep in the flowers, fanned
by the wings of painted butterflies. Shakspere's
fun breaks out in the endless blunderings of the
" Comedy of Errors " as well as in the " Merry
Wives of Windsor," which he wrote for Queen
Elizabeth herself. Though only a country-born
lad, he caught up the spirit of the times, and wrote
such tragedy and comedy as had not been written
since the days of olden Greece.

Let us take one of his stories and tell it shortly.

There was a rich Jew called Shylock living at
Venice. There was also a man named Antonio,
" one in whom the ancient Roman honour more
appeared than any that drew breath in Italy."
There was also a man called Bassanio, a friend
of Antonio's, who wanted to marry a wealthy
lady at Venice called Portia. Would Antonio
lend him some money so that he could marry ?
Now, Antonio was expecting some ships back
from the East laden with merchandise. So the
two friends went to Shylock, the rich Jew, and
asked him to advance some money which should
be repaid on the arrival of the ships. Shylock
offered a large sum of money, making only one
condition, half in jest, half in earnest, that if
the money were not paid on the appointed day,

Shylock should exact a pound of Antonio's flesh, to be cut where it pleased him. Antonio signed the bond, thinking it was only "merry sport," and took the money. So Bassanio married Portia. But that very same day they heard the sad news that Antonio's ships had been lost at sea, and that he could never now repay Shylock. He had therefore been cast into prison.

At once Bassanio and Portia set out in all haste for Venice, to save, if possible, the friend who was suffering for them. Portia knew how Bassanio loved his friend, how he would sacrifice "his life itself, his wife, and all the world" for him, and she now made a plan. She wrote to her cousin, who was going to judge Antonio at the trial, and begged to be allowed to plead instead. She dressed up in his robes of law and entered the court. Looking round, she saw the merciless Shylock, she saw Bassanio standing by Antonio in an agony of distress. Nobody recognised her, and the trial began. Her famous plea for mercy is one of Shakspere's finest passages, that mercy which "droppeth as the gentle rain from heaven upon the place beneath." But Shylock would have no mercy.

Antonio's bosom was bared for the knife, and the scales were ready to weigh the pound of flesh, when Portia cried,—

> "Tarry a little ; there is something else.
> This bond doth give thee here no jot of blood ;
> The words expressly are, a pound of flesh."

Now Shylock could not possibly take a pound of flesh without shedding blood, so by her clever action Portia saved the life of Antonio, her husband's friend. Shylock escaped, Antonio's ships came in after all, and the play ends happily with the joy of Portia and Bassanio.

Shakspere went on writing long after the death of Elizabeth. His plays grew very serious and thoughtful as life went on. In 1610 he returned from the noisy London theatres to the peace of Stratford-on-Avon, where a few years later he passed to

> " The undiscover'd country from whose bourne
> No traveller returns."

25. THE GOLDEN DAYS OF GOOD QUEEN BESS.

> " Upon this land a thousand, thousand blessings,
> Which time shall bring to ripeness."
> —SHAKSPERE.

AND what shall we say of this great queen, Elizabeth, in whose reign England first rose to be a world-power ?

At the age of twenty-five she had mounted the throne, at a moment when the fortunes of the country were low and the mighty empire of Spain was growing ever more and more mighty. At the age of seventy she died, leaving her country united and prosperous, with the power of Spain broken.

"Though you have had and may have many princes more mighty and wise sitting in this seat," were her last words to the people, "yet you never had any one that will be more careful and loving."

This was true. She had many faults, but she cared for England, and Englishmen rallied round her. With scanty means at her command, she succeeded in guiding England safely through the dangers which threatened her on every side. Freed from the power of Spain, the country began to realise her position with regard to the sea power of Europe. Men awoke to a sense of the great possibilities before their country, and they all worked to make her greater. But it was Elizabeth herself who made it all possible, she who "gave to each his opportunity."

Thus she had Drake for her great sea-captain, Raleigh for her courtier and colonist, Spenser for her poet, and Shakspere for her dramatist. She herself had been brought up amid the new culture of her father's Court. She could shoot and ride, she could dance and play, she was a good Greek scholar and spoke two foreign tongues.

Fourteen years old when her father died, she had seen her little ten-year-old brother, Edward VI., ascend the throne. On his death, six years later, she had ridden by the side of her sister Mary when she was proclaimed Queen of England. Mary's marriage with Philip of Spain[1] had brought

---

[1] See Book III. chapter 7.

the country to the verge of war, and it was perhaps well for England that her death, five years
later, set Elizabeth upon the throne.

The whole country, now at peace, broke out into
wonderful new life. Into the Old World was
poured the wealth of the New World. Spain
could no longer keep secret the riches of America.
English eyes were strained across the seas, English
hands were eagerly grasping the treasure that had
belonged to Spain and Portugal for years. For the
first time since Vasco da Gama[1] had sailed round
the Cape to India, and Columbus had discovered
America, Englishmen dashed aside the curtain
drawn by Spain and Portugal across their con-
quests in the East and West.

Contact with the New World brought commerce,
commerce brought money, money brought luxury.
Personal comforts increased. Carpets replaced the
dirty flooring of rushes used up to this time, pillows
came into general use, wooden plates were replaced
by metal or silver, glass windows adorned the new
houses and manors which sprang up all over the
country.

With new luxuries and comforts came a love of
beauty and display. The queen herself boasted of
having 3000 dresses in her wardrobe. Her courtiers
vied with one another in the splendour of ruffs and
velvet coats. The old ideas of thrift melted before
the fortunes made by adventurers sailing to the

[1] See Book II. chapter 31.

East or West. Visions of ships laden with pearls, diamonds, and gold dazzled the humblest sailor, while dreams of an El Dorado where everything was made of gold tempted the most indolent beyond the seas.

This love of travel quickened men's minds. England was ready for her great awakening. Poets burst forth into song, writers into prose. The full glory arose with Spenser and his "Fairy Queen." For two hundred years no great poem had broken the silence of English song. It expressed the Elizabethan age as no other poem had done. It did for poetry what William Shakspere did for the drama, representing

> "The very age and body of the time,
> Its form and pressure."

So all these men—adventurers, explorers, poets, dramatists, philosophers, and statesmen—helped to make Elizabeth's England great, splendid, triumphant; fit to take her place in the world's history, and to play the great part for which she was destined.

With the queen's death in 1603 the golden days ended for a time. But she had fulfilled the prophecy of Shakspere at her birth. She had showered upon the land

> "A thousand, thousand blessings,
> Which time shall bring to ripeness."

Good had grown with her, man had sung the "merry songs of peace to all his neighbours."

Peace, plenty, love, truth, strength—these were her servants. And Shakspere was but voicing the feelings of the queen when he speaks of—

" This blessed plot, this earth, this realm, this England,

This land of such dear souls, this dear dear land,

England, bound in with the triumphant sea."

26. FIRST VOYAGE OF THE EAST INDIA COMPANY.

"Whosoever commands the sea, commands the trade ; whosoever commands the trade of the world, commands the riches of the world, and consequently the world itself."—RALEIGH.

FAR away in the Arctic regions, on a map of the world, may be seen the name Davis Straits, given to a wide sea between the western coast of Greenland and North America. This sea was discovered by John Davis, one of Elizabeth's most famous explorers, a man who not only did good work among the ice - bound regions of the north, but also piloted the first English ship sent by the East India Company to trade with those distant lands, henceforth to form so large a part of the British Empire.

John Davis was a Devonshire lad, like so many of the sixteenth-century sailors. Humphrey Gilbert and Walter Raleigh were his lifelong friends;

Hawkins, Drake, and Frobisher, the inspirers of his boyish dreams.

Davis had been at sea some time himself when Frobisher sailed forth in the little Gabriel for the north-west passage, which attracted so many to that land of ice and peril. But it was not until Frobisher had given up his gallant work, to waste his efforts in the search after imaginary gold, that John Davis took up his work. To find a short cut to India by the north, by which English ships could sail to and fro without fear from the great Spanish vessels which haunted the Cape route—this was the dream of Davis.

Sailing early in January 1585 in two little ships, bearing the romantic names of Sunshine and Moonshine, he reached the coast of Greenland. And it was Davis who gave the most southern point of that cold land the name Cape Farewell, which it bears to-day.

Three times did he sail to the icy north, each time reaching a farther point and making fresh important discoveries. To him is due the honour of having re-discovered Greenland, which had been lost sight of since the days of the old Vikings, two centuries before. He also explored the sea known to us to-day as Davis Straits. He mapped out the mysterious regions of the north, and pointed out the way to those who came after. "He lighted Hudson into his strait. He lighted Baffin into his bay." But he did more than this. By his true-

hearted devotion to the cause of Arctic discovery,
by his patient research, his dauntless enthusiasm,
he set an example which became a beacon-light to
northern explorers of all time.

But his last voyage to the north was not successful, and the owners of the ships under his charge
turned their eyes to India by way of the Cape of
Good Hope, instead of dreaming of a shorter way
by the perilous and ice-bound north.

The destruction of the Spanish Armada had made
the voyage for English ships by the Cape less
hazardous than before. England had swept away
for a time the fleets of Spain and Portugal, and
could now undertake safely the long sea route by
South Africa in order to bring back rich cargoes
from India and the islands beyond.

These merchant ships had heretofore been fitted
out by private people, who bought the ships, appointed the commander, and received the reward.
Now the merchant-princes of England made up
their minds to join together in a company, to fit
out fleets and establish direct trade with India,
sharing the profits.

The queen approved of the arrangement, and
on the very last day of the sixteenth century
the East India Company, as it was called, was
started. Soon a little fleet of ships left England
under direction of the Company; and the chief
pilot of the fleet was our old friend of the Arctic
Seas, John Davis, on board the Red Dragon.

He had but just returned from piloting two Dutch ships, the Lion and the Lioness, under Cornelius Houtman, to Malacca by the Cape of Good Hope, for which services he had been specially thanked.

"The Dutch had special assistance in their late navigations by the means of Master John Davis, and in return the Dutch do in ample manner requite us, acquainting us with their voyages, discoveries, and dangers, both outward and homeward."

His services were now required by his own countrymen, for this was a memorable voyage, inasmuch as it laid the foundation of the British Empire in the East.

The ships returned triumphantly from this first expedition under the Company, to be received by the news that Queen Elizabeth was dead, that James I. was on the English throne, and that a Dutch East India Company had been formed to rival English trade with India and the East.

27. THE STORY OF HENRY HUDSON.

"To achieve what they have undertaken, or else to give reason wherefore it will not be."—HENRY HUDSON.

A DUTCH East India Company had been formed, and one of its most daring servants was an Englishman, Henry Hudson. His name can never be forgotten, for it is written large on every map of the world. There is Hudson Bay in North America; Hudson river, on which New York now stands; Hudson Strait,—all of which remind us of one of the bravest and ablest seamen that ever lived. The story of his success in the frozen north, his patient endurance of hardships, and his tragic death in the waters of the bay he himself had discovered, is a thrilling one in the annals of the sea.

Henry Hudson first makes his appearance as a sea-captain in 1607, leaving London with the intention of finding a passage to China by the frozen seas of the north. The merchants of London, in spite of failure, were still bent on finding a northern passage to the lands of spice and gold which were enriching Spain and Portugal. Frobisher and Davis had tried in vain to find a way to the north-west. Other men, notably the Dutchman Barentz and the Englishman Willoughby, had failed to find a passage by the north-east.

Now a bolder scheme arose. Was there a sailor daring enough to sail over the mysterious north pole itself to reach the other side? Yes. Henry Hudson was willing to try. And in a tiny ship, with a scanty crew, he sailed away on his adventurous voyage to the frozen seas. A fortnight later he had reached Greenland. The weather was thick and foggy, and his sails and ropes were soon frozen hard. He tried to sail to the north, but a barrier of ice blocked his way. Sailing along this barrier he reached Spitzbergen. Again and again he tried to find a way through the ice and snow to reach the north pole. But winter was coming on, he had already explored farther north than any one else, and he reluctantly turned homewards. Among other pieces of news, he brought home information of the whales he had seen in the seas about Spitzbergen, thus starting the whale-fishing, which was a great source of wealth to England.

A second expedition failed to discover any possible passage to China, though Hudson reached Nova Zembla and explored that region. The sailors brought back a story of how they had seen a mermaid. She came close to the ship's side, they said, and looked earnestly at them. Then the sea came and overturned her. Her skin was white, and long black hair hung down behind. As she went down they saw her tail, which was like the tail of a porpoise and speckled like a mackerel. The creature they saw was probably a seal, but the idea took the fancy of the poets and story-tellers.

Hudson's third voyage was made in the service of the Dutch East India Company. He left Amsterdam in a ship called the Good Hope, with a crew of mixed English and Dutch. Failing to get farther to the north, Hudson sailed for the shores of North America. Having touched at Newfoundland and seeing " a great fleet of Frenchmen fishing on the bank," he sailed along the coast, partly looking for the English colony of Virginia, partly seeking some passage to the west. While cruising thus he discovered the Hudson river. Here is his own account :—

" The sun rose and we saw the land all like broken islands. We then came to a great lake of water, looking like a drowned land. The mouth of that land hath many shoals, and the sea breaketh on them. It is a very good land to fall in with, and a pleasant land to see. At 3 of the clock in the afternoon we came to three great rivers, where we saw many salmons and mullets, very great.

" We found a very good harbour, and went in with our ship. Then we took our nets to fish, and caught ten great mullets and a ray as great as four men could haul into the ship. The people of the country seemed glad of our coming and brought green tobacco. They dress in deer-skins. They have a great store of maize, whereof they make good bread. We now turned into the river. It is a mile broad, and there is high land on both sides."

Sailing, rowing, and fishing, anchoring by night to keep a careful watch on the treacherous natives, Hudson went some hundred miles up the great river that was to bear his name—the river on which to-day stands New York, the largest city in America.

He brought home news, too, of an opening to the west, which he wished to explore farther.

Yet a fourth time we find Hudson leaving home. This time in an English ship called the Discovery, which brought him safely to the other side of the Atlantic Ocean. It was for the last time. He had intended to strike the coast of America near the Hudson river, but contrary winds and icebergs drove the ship out of her course, through an unknown strait, into a great inland sea. Both of these waters still bear the explorer's name—Hudson Strait and Hudson Bay.

Day after day the little ship sailed on, but no opening could be seen by which they could escape from the ice-bound sea which they had unknowingly entered. For three months they tried, but in vain. Then winter overtook them. "The nights were long and cold and the ground was covered with snow." Food was scarce and the sailors grew dissatisfied. The ice broke up at last, and Hudson still hoped to find a passage to the west. But now the sailors rose in mutiny.

"We would rather be hanged at home than starved abroad," they cried drearily. In order to make the food last longer they bound their brave captain and forced him with his son and a few sick men into an open boat. And then, amid that icy sea, far away from friends and home, with no food and no human help, they cast Henry Hudson adrift. At the last moment the carpenter sprang into the drifting boat, resolved to die with his captain rather than desert him. The little boat and its starving crew were never heard of again. Henry Hudson, one of the bravest and most daring of English seamen, must have found a grave in the icy waters of the very inland sea he had discovered.

He had done much. He gave to England the fisheries of Spitzbergen and the fur-trade of Hudson Bay, as well as the vast tract of country between that bay and the Pacific Ocean. He gave to Holland the colony at the mouth of the Hudson river, which they called New Amsterdam, but which under the English became New York, its name to-day.

One more expedition was made some six years later, and then for two hundred years the lonely solitude of those ice-bound regions remained unbroken.

28. CAPTAIN JOHN SMITH.

"To the West! To the West! To the land of the free,
Where the mighty Missouri rolls down to the sea,
Where a man is a man, if he's willing to toil,
And the humblest may gather the fruits of the soil."
—MACKAY.

FAILURE after failure had attended the early efforts of the English to plant colonies in the West. Still they would not give up.

"I shall yet live to see Virginia an English nation," the far-sighted Raleigh had said even when the news had reached him of the pathetic end of his little colony.

But it was not till the power of Spain had been destroyed that the English could hope to succeed in America. For an infant colony is like an army at the end of a long line of communications. If the line is cut, it must perish. Before England could plant thriving colonies in America she had to gain control of the ocean-paths leading across the Atlantic. Now this was done. The defeat of the Spanish Armada had made American colonisation possible to England.

And so in 1606 another infant colony, consisting of 105 persons, sailed from "merrie England" for Virginia, the "paradise of the world" as the poets loved to call it. Queen Elizabeth was dead, but James I. was ready enough for a chance of extending his dominions beyond the seas. The emigrants sailed in three small ships, which took four long months to reach the shores of America. They had intended to land on the coast of Virginia, but a great storm drove them out of their course, and they found themselves in a magnificent bay, called by the natives Chesapeake Bay. Landing on the banks of a river, which they called James river, after the king, they decided on a suitable site for a colony, which they called Jamestown. They began to build, but it was soon evident that

the wrong stamp of colonist had come out. Out
of the 105 emigrants there were but twelve
labouring men ; the others were gentlemen, unused
to toil, unfit for hardships. Again and again the
Indians attacked them.

Then came the old story—food ran short, disease
followed, three or four died daily, and the survivors
were too weak to bury them. At last half the
little colony was dead.

Among the colonists was a young man called
John Smith. He was strong and vigorous, and
he saw something must be done. So he undertook to rule them. He first strengthened the town
against attacks from the Indians, and, to get fresh
supplies of food, he led parties to explore the neighbourhood. He cheered the few survivors, and all
went well for a time, till one day Smith himself
was attacked and taken prisoner by the Indians.
He was led before the chief and doomed to death.
For a time he warded off the evil moment by ex-
plaining the mariner's compass and telling the
ignorant natives stories.

"And when I told them the wonders of the
earth and sky and spheres, of the sun and moon
and stars, and how the sun did chase the night
round the world continually, they all stood amazed
with admiration," said John Smith when he wrote
of all his strange adventures with the Indians.
But when his stories came to an end, all their
fury burst forth again, and tying him to a tree,

they prepared their arrows to shoot him. Another moment he would have been a dead man, when the chief stepped forward and bade them unbind the prisoner, who was to be taken before Powhatan, the king of the tribe.

From one village to another he was now led in triumph—the only white man among all the Indians — till at length he reached the king. The old chieftain was sitting before a fire on a bench. He was covered with skins of animals, whose tails hung around him like tassels. Near him sat a row of women, their faces and bare shoulders painted bright red. Smith thought he was well received, for the queen brought him water to wash his hands and a bunch of feathers to dry them instead of a towel.

But preparations to kill him now went forward. Two large stones were brought in, on which the unhappy Englishman was made to lay his head. Two dusky warriors stood, with clubs upraised, waiting the word to strike, when suddenly the king's little daughter of ten years old darted forward, laid her young head upon his, and thus saved his life. The king was deeply touched by this act of devotion on the part of his child Pocahontas. He at once set his prisoner free, and sent him back to Jamestown under escort.

He found the colonists reduced to forty now, and they were in the act of leaving when Smith arrived and once more saved the situation. Thanks to Pocahontas, there was now peace with the Indians, and food came in regularly. Moreover, they taught the colonists many things—how to grow maize and how to till the ground. Emigrants now poured over from England.

"When you send again, I entreat you send me thirty carpenters, husbandmen, gardeners, fishermen, and blacksmiths, rather than a thousand such as these," Smith wrote home pitifully. He made a rule that every one must work for six hours a-day at least.

"He who will not work, shall not eat," he said. But the axes blistered their tender hands till the sound of oaths drowned the echo of the blows. To put down this swearing Smith decreed that every oath should be punished by a can of cold water being poured down the swearer's sleeve, which was the cause of much merriment and fewer oaths.

So John Smith succeeded where others had failed. He was the first to show that the true interest of England was not to seek gold in Virginia, as the early colonists had done, but rather, by patient toil and unwearying industry, to establish trade and commerce.

"Nothing," he used to say—"nothing is to be expected from thence but by labour."

The sequel to this story is interesting. Pocahontas became a Christian and married one of the colonists, John Rolfe, at Jamestown, and in 1616 she went to England with her husband. She had been the first native in America to become a Christian, and her romantic story drew crowds to see her. "La Belle Sauvage" was taken to the Court of King James by John Smith himself, who was in England at the time. But she had not been in England long before she was taken very ill, and she died before she could be put on board ship to return to her native country.

29. THE FOUNDING OF QUEBEC.

"Row, brothers, row, the stream runs fast,
The Rapids are near, and the daylight's past."
—T. MOORE, *Canadian Boat Song.*

WHILE Henry Hudson was sailing up his newly discovered river, and the little colony of Virginia was growing daily stronger under Captain John Smith, other countries were busy colonising on the shores of the New World. If there was a New England and a New Holland over the seas, there was also a New France.

Some sixty years before this time, when the spirit of discovery was abroad and all eyes were turned towards the golden East, a French sailor called Jacques Cartier left his native shores to try and find a new passage to India by way of America. His home was at St Malo, a seaport in Brittany—the nursery of hardy mariners such as himself. In the town hall there to-day hangs his portrait, the keen eyes ever searching something beyond the seas that dashed against the shores of his native town.

He left France in the summer of 1534 with three small ships, and sailed across the Atlantic Ocean to the storm-beaten shores of Labrador, already discovered by Cabot. Passing through the narrow straits between that coast and Newfoundland, he came to a great expanse of water, which he named the Bay of St Lawrence, a name he gave later to the great river which flows into this mighty bay. Undaunted by the dangers of the unknown, Jacques Cartier, with two young natives, made his way up the river St Lawrence till he came to some great cliffs standing high above the surging current below. Little did he think, as he looked at those silent heights, that here should be the site of the busy city of Quebec[1] in Canada, now full of heroic memories. At this time only a cluster of rude huts crowned the summit of the rock. But this little native village was not the capital of the forest state, so the Indians told the French sailor.

On the banks of the river, some days' journey hence, stood the great native town called Hochelaga. In a little boat, with fifty sailors, Cartier set out for the mysterious city. Forests with trees thickly hung with grapes lined the shores

[1] See Book IV. chapter 7.

of the river up which they now rowed, the water
was alive with wildfowl, the air rang with the
song of blackbird and thrush. As they neared
the city, Indians thronged the shore. Wild with
delight, dancing, singing, crowding round the
strangers, they threw into the boat presents of
fish and maize. As it grew dark, fires were lit,
and the Frenchmen could see the excited natives
still leaping and dancing by the blaze. When
day dawned Cartier followed his guides by a
forest path to Hochelaga. Beneath the oaks of
the forest the ground was thickly strewn with
acorns. Before him rose a great mountain, at the
foot of which lay the Indian town. Swarms of
natives now rushed round the white men, touching
their beards and feeling their faces.

"We will call the mountain here Mont Royal,"
said Jacques Cartier, and the name survives in
Montreal, to-day one of the busiest cities in
Canada.

It would take too long to tell of Jacques
Cartier's return down the river, how winter came
on him suddenly and hemmed him in until the
river itself froze over and the whole earth was
deeply wrapped in snow. He returned to France
in course of time, with his account of the two
native villages built on the river St Lawrence.

Cartier had discovered. It was for another man
to build and colonise. This man was Champlain,
known as the "Father of New France." And he

did more than build, he sailed farther up the
river and discovered Lake Ontario and the famous rapids, now known as the Falls of Niagara
(Thunder of Waters.)

In the year 1603 Champlain found himself at
the mouth of the St Lawrence river, anxious to
examine the native villages of which Cartier had
brought such glowing reports. For some unknown
reason all was now silent and deserted. He passed
under the bare rock of Quebec and made his way
to the once populous village of Hochelaga. But
all signs of life were gone since the days of Jacques
Cartier. As he rowed back, the rugged charm of
the place seized his fancy. He saw the broad river,
the good seaport, the thick forests in their varying
hues, and the idea of building cities on the native
sites appealed strongly to him. Five years later
he was ready, and sailed from France with men,
arms, and stores for a colony on the banks of the
river St Lawrence.

On a level piece of land between the summit of
the cliffs and the river, where a cluster of native
huts had once stood, Champlain chose his site.
The woodmen were soon engaged in making a
clearing, and in a few weeks a pile of wooden
buildings had arisen just where the busy city of
Quebec now stands. Very soon winter was upon
them. They must stand by their colony, though
building should be impossible through the frost
and snow. With twenty - eight men Champlain

prepared to hold the settlement. Sadly he watched the many-tinted autumn leaves fall from the forest trees; the sunshine of October faded, and November brought a bare waste of country. The river froze over, and soon a heavy blanket of snow buried the earth. The winters of Canada are very long, and it was May before anything further could be done. By this time twenty men out of twenty-eight were dead, and the others were all suffering from illness, when a welcome sail appeared on the river below with help and food. Champlain was now free to found another trading station at the Mont Royal of Cartier— the Montreal of to-day.

For twenty-seven years he toiled ceaselessly to build up the New France beyond the seas, and the early history of Canada is centred in the life-story of Champlain, the Father of New France. Quebec and Montreal were active centres of French trade, until they passed into English hands; and it is but a few years ago that an Englishman unveiled a statue of Champlain in the very heart of the city he had founded nearly three hundred years ago.

30. THE PILGRIM FATHERS.

" Go, and in regions far such heroes bring ye forth
  As those from whom we came ; and plant our name
  Under that star not known unto our north."
                              —MICHAEL DRAYTON.

UNDER James I., King of England, there was a little sect of Protestants, known as Puritans, who were sorely persecuted. They were very strict in their ideas of worship. They wished everything to be more Lutheran. They thought it wrong to amuse themselves. It was, in their eyes, a sin to hunt, a sin to put starch into a ruff, to play at chess.

At last a little band of these Puritans made up their minds to sail over to Holland, "where," they heard, " was freedom of religion for all men." They hoped in a new land, among new people, to spread their views, and, at any rate, to be left in peace. So across the sea to Holland they went, arriving at Amsterdam in the year 1608. For twelve years they lived at Leyden among the Dutch ; but they lived as exiles in a strange land, and Puritanism did not spread as they had hoped. So they turned their eyes across the seas to the New World, where colonisation was now going on apace. There they might preach their Puritan gospel ; there, on the shores of the New World, they might start life afresh.

Now the Dutch people had grown very fond of the English Puritans.

"These English," they said, "have lived among us for twelve years, and yet we have not anything to say against one of them."

It was the summer of 1620 when the Puritans left Leyden for the New World. A crowd was waiting by the shore to see these Pilgrim Fathers off. In floods of tears the Dutch bade farewell to these people they had learnt to love, and they were not able to speak for their sorrow.

"But the tide, which stays for no man," bore the Pilgrim Fathers away, and with a fair wind the little ship reached Southampton, where two larger ships, the Mayflower and the Speedwell, awaited them. Here there were many delays, and it was late in the summer before the ships left the shores of England. The Speedwell soon put back, and only the little Mayflower, with forty-one emigrants and their families, was left to face the perils of the great Atlantic Ocean. It was not long before great gales set in, and the long swell of the Atlantic almost washed over the little ship. Still the Mayflower went forward, struggling gallantly with wind and weather. Once or twice the poor Pilgrims were tempted to turn and go home, so great was the misery of those on board. They were terribly crowded together, sea-sick, and frightened at the high waves which broke over the little ship, but still they went forward.

So sixty-four days passed away on a voyage which now takes about a week, when early one November morning the Pilgrims first caught sight of America. Together they rejoiced and praised God, "that had given them once again to see the land."

The low sandhills of Cape Cod seemed a very haven of rest to the poor storm-beaten Pilgrims. Their voyage, indeed, was at an end, but the prospect before them was dreary enough. The wintry wind howled through the battered little ship, and its icy blasts went through the thin frames of the old Pilgrims, worn by hardship and sickness.

Sixteen of them were put ashore to find a suitable place to settle. These landed and marched wearily about, through sandy woods, sleeping amid forests; but, finding no place for a settlement, they returned sadly to the ship. Then they explored the coast. The weather grew very cold, the salt spray of the sea froze upon their clothes, so that they seemed cased all over as in coats of iron.

At last they left Cape Cod and landed in Plymouth Bay, so called from the last place they had left in England. There was plenty of fish here, springs of water and good harbours. So, leaving the women and children on board, they began to lay out streets and houses. But the winter was on them, and they had already borne all they could.

One by one they sickened, one by one they died, till only half the little band was left.

At last the warm spring days followed the bitter winter weather, and the Pilgrims, under their stout-hearted leader Miles Standish, took fresh hope. They made friends with the Indians, they tilled the soil and planted seeds from England.

Then there came a day, nearly four months after their landing, when the Mayflower must go back to England. She had been riding at anchor in the bay, "battered and blackened and worn by all the storms of the winter."

Here is the heroism of the story. Not one of the Pilgrims went home in her.

" O strong hearts and true, not one went back in the Mayflower ;
  No, not one looked back who set his hand to the ploughing."

With overflowing eyes they stood on the sea-shore watching with heavy hearts the homeward-bound ship as she bounded over the waters, leaving them alone in the desert.

" Lost in the sound of the oars was the last farewell of the
  Pilgrims."

Months and years of hardships followed, but resolutely they worked and toiled, and slowly things grew better. A shipful of friends followed them from England. In ten years there were 300 settlers ; every year the numbers grew until, forty-two years later, it became part of that State now known as

Massachusetts. In that Plymouth across the seas a statue now stands marking the spot where the Pilgrim Fathers landed all these long years ago. Their heroism and perseverance were never forgotten.

"Let it not grieve you that you have broken the ice for others who come after," said their English friends. "The honour shall be yours to the world's end."

31. THIRTY YEARS OF WAR.

"It is without example
In the world's history."
—SCHILLER.

WHILE the Pilgrim Fathers were building their new homes on the shores of America, the eyes of Europe were turned towards Germany, where war had broken out. It was destined to be one of the most terrible wars waged in modern times. This feud between the Protestants and Roman Catholics of Germany had long been simmering ; but the great armed struggle finally broke forth on May 23, 1618, and continued till it had drawn nearly every European nation into its conflict, till it had lighted the fires of battle from the Baltic to the Mediterranean Seas.

To follow the war through all its many phases would be impossible, but two great names stand out from amid the waste of war, names among the most famous in the world's history—Wallenstein and Gustavus Adolphus. The war had raged for fourteen years when these two great generals met on the battlefield of Lützen. They had never met in battle before. They were never to meet again. A greater contrast than these two famous commanders never existed.

Wallenstein, fighting on the side of the Catholics, was cold, gloomy, silent. Ambition was the ruling power of his life.

"I must command alone or not at all," he had once said. All men stood in awe of him. He was a rich landowner, and raised armies at his own expense for the emperor; but "God help the land to which these men come!" said a frightened German who had just watched Wallenstein's troops marching past.

Gustavus Adolphus, King of Sweden, was a very different man. Frank and fearless, he was a staunch Protestant and the very idol of his own people. He now came forward to defend the liberty of his country and the Protestant religion, which both seemed in danger from Germany. Landing on the northern coast of Germany in a storm of thunder and lightning, he had been the first to leap ashore and to kneel in thanks to God for his safe passage.

"A good Christian can never be a bad soldier," he said as he led his men forward. As he passed through German territory men flocked to his stand-

ard ; they even knelt before him, struggling for
the honour of touching the sheath of his sword or
the hem of his garment.

" This people would make a king of me," he said
sadly. " My God knoweth that I have no delight
in it. Soon enough shall be revealed my human
weakness."

Nevertheless his march through the Protestant
states of Germany was like a triumphal procession,
and tears of relief and joy streamed down the
cheeks of bearded men as they welcomed this
" Lion of the North," who had come to deliver
the oppressed Protestants.

Gustavus Adolphus had reached the very heart
of the nation. No wonder the emperor became
alarmed and turned to Wallenstein, the only
leader at all capable of measuring swords with
the King of Sweden. Wallenstein answered his
emperor's call. As if by magic he collected an
enormous army. His military fame drew men of
all nations to his banner. From north and south,
from east and west, they came. " All swarm to
the old familiar long-loved banner," and

> " Yet one sole man can rein this fiery host
>   By equal rule, by equal love and fear
>   Blending the many-nationed whole in one."

It was in November 1632 that this mixed army
under Wallenstein found itself at Lützen, a small
town in Germany. The winter was coming on

and Wallenstein was moving into winter quarters, hoping his rival would do the same, when he heard that Gustavus Adolphus was marching on Lützen— indeed that he was near even now.

Through the long dark night the Swedish army had been marching, till with the first streaks of dawn, when they had intended to surprise Wallenstein, they found a thick fog hiding everything from view.

Kneeling in front of his army, the king burst into Luther's hymn, "God is a strong tower," following it with his own battle-song, which began,

> "Be not dismayed, thou little flock."

Some of his officers begged Gustavus to clothe himself in steel, after the custom of the age.

"God is my armour," he cried, throwing it aside.

So he wore only a plain cloth coat and a buff waistcoat, which may be seen at Vienna to-day.

Toward eleven o'clock the sun burst forth, and the two armies could almost see the battle-light that glowed fiercely in each other's eyes. The Swedish king gave his last orders. Then drawing his sword and waving it above his head, he advanced with the Swedish war-cry: "God with us!"

"It will now be shown whether I or the King of Sweden is to be master of the world," said Wallenstein gloomily, as he led his men to the battle.

They had not fought long when the fog came down once more, and Gustavus dashed unawares into a regiment of the enemy. One shot passed through his horse, another shattered his own arm and wounded him in the back. He fell to the ground.

" Who are you ? " asked one of his foes.

" I *was* the King of Sweden," gasped the dying king, and murmuring to himself, " My God ! my God ! " he died.

As the mournful tidings ran through the Swedish army it nerved the men to fresh effort. They cared not for their lives, now the most precious life had passed. With the fury of lions they rushed on the foe, and when the sun set that November night Wallenstein, defeated at last, was in full retreat.

Gustavus Adolphus, the great champion of Protestantism, was dead, but his men had won the victory as he would have had them do. They dragged a great stone to the place where their hero fell, and on it they wrote the words, " Our faith is the victory which overcometh the world."

Wallenstein was assassinated two years after this great battle. Years later peace was made, and there has never been a war of religion in Europe since those days.

32. THE DUTCH AT SEA.

"To navigate is necessary, to live is not."—*Motto of the
Hanseatic League.*

THE Thirty Years' War was over. A general peace
had been made, which included most of the nations
of Europe. Holland and Spain made peace, too,
after long years of fighting, and the King of Spain
admitted that Holland was now free—no longer
dependent on Spain.

The little country reclaimed from the sea had
never been so great before. She made the most
of her opportunity, and soon rose to be foremost
amid all the nations of Europe. Ever a seafaring people, it was now to the sea that they
again turned. Commerce was almost as necessary
to Holland as the religious liberty for which she
had fought so long. Since the days when the
Beggars of the Sea had taken Brille, and the
fireships of Antwerp had helped in the defeat of
the Spanish Armada, her sea-power had been
rapidly growing. If England had formed an East
India Company, Holland had followed her quickly
with a Dutch East India Company. And even
before the death of Sir Walter Raleigh her ships
had outwitted those of England.

"The Hollanders send into France, Spain,
Portugal, and Italy," he cried to his king, "with
Baltic produce about 2000 merchant ships, and

we have none. They traffic into every city and port around about this land with five or six hundred ships, and we into three towns in their country with forty ships."

So the ships of Holland grew and multiplied; they were better and faster than the English; they had ousted the Portuguese from their strong positions in the East. To carry on better their trade with India and the Spice Islands, the Dutch had built themselves a town in the Island of Java. It was like a miniature Amsterdam, with its busy dockyards, its crowded wharfs, its shaded canals, and its huge warehouses. Indeed it was built upon a swamp and called after their old country, Batavia. It soon became the headquarters of the Dutch East India Company, and is to-day the centre of the Dutch colonial empire.

Here, at Batavia, they shipped the spices which made their country so wealthy. It is hard to understand how eagerly our forefathers loved these Eastern spices. Ginger, pepper, mace, nut-megs—these were always in great demand, and at feasts in Europe a seat near the spice-box was the seat of honour.

The sale of these spices brought untold wealth into Holland, as they would let no one else sell them. So the Dutch people bought nutmegs at 4d. per lb. in the East to sell them at 3s. per lb. in Europe. Pepper, which cost 2½d. per lb. out there, was sold at nearly 2s. elsewhere.

Not only did they sail to the East, but also to the West.   One day a Dutch admiral, Piet Hein, chased some Spanish ships in the Atlantic.   They were bringing home to Spain a rich cargo of silver from Mexico, all of which Piet Hein captured.

> " Piet Hein.   Short is his name.
>   But great is his fame,
>   For the silver fleet he's ta'en,"

sang his countrymen as they stored their riches at Amsterdam.

All their riches and merchandise the Dutch stored at Amsterdam.   There they built warehouses supported on piles driven into the swampy soil, in which they stowed the treasures of the world, until Amsterdam was the most famous city in Europe.

Not only was Holland teaching the rest of the world the value of the sea, but she was teaching them how to make more of the land.   As soon as peace had come to the country the people had begun to reclaim more land for cultivation.   They pumped and pumped till they had got a great piece of rich meadow-land from what had been a vast shallow lake of water.   The cattle grazing on this land became the finest in Europe ; the produce of Dutch dairies found a ready market in foreign countries.

Then, too, their market-gardens were better than any of their neighbours.   They cultivated and exported potatoes and turnips nearly a century before England.   They discovered the use of clover and improved grasses for fodder.

Keen as they were after profit to be obtained by trade, diligent in working out the resources of their country, they were also distinguished in art, literature, and painting. They had their artists in Rembrandt and Vandyke, their poet in Vondel.

Toward the end of the seventeenth century the Dutch were more famous by land and sea than any other nation in Europe. They were also the first to colonise the Cape of Good Hope, on the site now occupied by Cape Town.

33. THE GREAT SOUTH LAND.

"We looked upon a world unknown."—WHITTIER.

AT the beginning of the seventeenth century the vast ocean south of America, Africa, and Asia was unknown; there was a blank space on the old charts where Australia is now marked. As men in the days of Columbus [1] had guessed at the great country on the far side of the Atlantic Ocean, so now they suspected some large tract of land to lie south of the equator—the Great South Land they called it vaguely, or Australia, from a word *Austral*, meaning south.

Many a Spaniard had left the shores of Peru in search of it, but up to this time with little result. Now that the Dutch had entered on their

[1] See Book II. chapter 35.

career of discovery in the East, it was natural that they in their turn should search for that unknown land.

In 1606 a Dutch ship sailed along part of the coast of Australia, but whenever the men landed they were driven away by wild savages with clubs. They called the headland that marked the limit of their voyage Cape Keer Weer, or Turnagain, which name it bears to-day. So ship after ship sailed to the coast of Australia under the Dutch East India Company.

In 1642 an expedition was despatched from Batavia, the headquarters of the Company, under the command of Captain Tasman, on a voyage of discovery to the Great South Land. Let him tell his own story.

"On August 14, 1642, I sailed from Batavia with two vessels," he says in his log-book, "and on September 5 anchored at Maurice Island, which has a very fine harbour. The country is mountainous, but the mountains are covered with green trees. The tops of these mountains are so high that they are lost in the clouds. The finest ebony in the world grows here. It is a tall, straight tree covered with a green bark, very thick, under which the wood is as black as pitch and as close as ivory. I left this island on the 8th of October and continued my course to the south. The weather was foggy, with hard gales and a rolling sea from the south.

" On November 24 I discovered land, which I called

Van Diemen's Land, after the Governor of Batavia, and on December 1 I anchored in a bay. I heard the sound of people on the shore, but I saw nobody. I perceived in the sand the mark of wild beasts' feet, resembling those of a tiger. We did nothing more here than set up a post, on which every one cut his name or his mark, and upon which I hoisted a flag.

"On December 5 I quitted Van Diemen's Land and steered east. On the 13th I discovered a high mountainous country. I coasted along the shore and anchored in a fine bay. We found here abundance of inhabitants: they had very hoarse voices and were very large-made people. They durst not approach the ship nearer than a stone's-throw, and we often observed them playing on a kind of trumpet. These people were of a colour between brown and yellow; their hair was long, combed up, and fixed at the top of their heads with a quill. On the 19th of December these savages began to grow a little bolder, insomuch that at last they ventured on board in order to trade with one of our vessels. Fearful lest they should surprise the ship, I sent a small boat with seven men to put the sailors on their guard. My seven men being without arms, were attacked by the savages, who killed three and forced the other four to swim for their lives: from which we called that place the Bay of Murderers.

"This country appeared to us rich, fertile, and well

situated; but as the weather was very foul, and we had at this time a very strong west wind, we continued our route to the north.

" On January 4, 1643, we sailed to a cape (Cape Maria Van Diemen), where we found the sea rolling in from the north-east, whence we concluded we had at last found a passage, which gave us no small joy.

" There was in this strait an island, which we called the Three Kings. Here we would have refreshed ourselves, but as we approached it we perceived on the mountain some thirty persons, men of very large size and each with a club in his hand. They called to us in a rough strong voice, but we could not understand what they said. They walked at a very great rate and took prodigious large strides. On January 21 we drew near to the coast of two islands, which we named Amsterdam and Rotterdam. Upon the island of Rotterdam we found plenty of hogs, fowls, and other refreshments. The people were good-natured, parting readily with what they had, and did not seem to know the use of arms."

From here Tasman sailed among many small islands surrounded with shoals and rocks, known as the Friendly Islands, until he returned to Batavia by the northern coast of New Guinea.

Not only had he discovered New Zealand, but he had sailed right round the vast unknown island of Australia without knowing it.

Some years later, when William III. was King of England, a brave sea-captain named Dampier was sent to further examine the shores of that great south land then known as New Holland. He found the country inhospitable, the natives " the most unpleasant and worst-featured of any people " he had ever seen.

After this the shores of Australia seem to have been forgotten for nearly a hundred years, when Captain Cook [1] made his famous discoveries and took possession of the country in the name of England.

34. VAN RIEBEEK'S COLONY.

" All the past we leave behind ;
We debouch upon a newer, mightier world, varied world.
Fresh and strong the world we seize, world of labour and the
    march,
        Pioneers ! O Pioneers ! "
                —WALT WHITMAN.

THE Dutch were now the chief carriers of the world, " waggoners of the sea," and their ships were constantly passing round the Stormy Cape on their way to and from Batavia. No longer did the Portuguese sail to and from the East as they had done of old. They had no Vasco da Gama, no Albuquerque, to lead them again to golden Goa.[2] Portugal, once the pioneer of navi-

---

[1] See Book IV. chapter 11.   [2] See Book II. chapter 34.

gation, now lay quiet, nerveless, crushed, and she has never since risen to play any large part in the world's history.

But the Dutch ships had much farther to go than had the Portuguese, and for some time past they had been in the habit of putting in to Table Bay, to take in fresh water on their long voyage to the East. These old Dutch ships, the quickest in the world then, took about 120 days, instead of twenty, to sail from Holland to the Cape. And they stood sorely in need of refreshment at the end of that time.

One day in the year 1649 a ship, the Haarlem, —one of the finest of Dutch ships,—was driven by a gale upon the beach at Table Bay. Her crew managed to save the cargo, but the ship became a total wreck. There was nothing to do now but to await the Dutch fleet, which would return shortly from Batavia. The crew under two men, Janssen and Proot, then explored the country, finally encamping on a site near the centre of the present city of Cape Town. They had saved some seeds and garden tools from the wreck, and soon a plot of ground was under cultivation. Cabbages, pumpkins, turnips, onions, and other vegetables grew splendidly; natives traded in friendship, bringing cattle and sheep; game fell to their guns, and fish was plentiful. Added to this, there was a stream of pure water, and the climate was delightful.

Van Riebeek's arrival at the Cape.

With the return fleet they sailed home to Holland to tell their countrymen of their experiment. A station was greatly needed somewhere in that region, and two years later a party of colonists left Holland to make a settlement on the shores of Table Bay. Jan van Riebeek was in command. He had been a great sailor and seen many countries, including the Cape. There were three ships, one of which was called the Goede Hoop, and on Christmas Day in. the year 1651 the little fleet sailed for South Africa.

It was Sunday morning, April 7, that Van Riebeek and his colonists looked for the first time upon the site of their future home. A suitable spot for the new fort was soon chosen, and building began at once. The new fort, called Good Hope, was in the form of a square, with very thick walls of earth, round which was a moat. A square tower rose to some height, from which the defenders could fire down upon any enemy who might attempt to scramble up the banks of earth. They built a hospital, where sick men from the ships could be left to recover, and a cattle-kraal to enclose the cattle bought from the natives.

Such was the original fort Good Hope, built by the Dutch in 1652 as a half-way house between the mother country and the Far East.

Like all the other early colonists, Van Riebeek and his settlers were doomed to suffer. The cold stormy winter set in about May, the heavy rain

poured through their tents, bringing sickness in
its train, and soon, out of the original 116 men,
only sixty were fit for work. They could get
no fresh meat save hippopotamus. They were as
solitary as the Pilgrim Fathers had been, thirty
years before, on the shores of North America.
But with spring dawned a new life. The grass
began to grow. Hendrik Boom, the gardener,
sowed his seeds, and soon there were plenty of
fresh vegetables, green grass for the cattle and
sheep, and fresh life for the home-sick colonists
in news from Holland brought by passing ships.

One day—it was January 18, 1653—a ship
came sailing hastily into Table Bay bringing the
news that war had been declared between Holland
and England. One can see the eager colonists
crowding round the Dutch sea-captain as he told
them all the news, for which they thirsted.

They knew there was no king in England at
this time, but that the country was in the hands
of a great man called Oliver Cromwell. It was
this Cromwell who had now made the famous
Navigation Act, which was aimed against Holland.
It decreed that English ships alone might bring
goods into England. Thus the trade of England
would be increased, but at the expense of Holland,
already supreme in the world of trade and commerce.
So the long rivalry of the two sea-going nations
had ended in a declaration of war. The little
colony at the Cape must strengthen its garrison

without delay, and the Dutch ship must sail on quickly to Batavia to warn the Dutch there of possible danger.

Meanwhile let us see what was really happening in England.

35. IN THE DAYS OF OLIVER CROMWELL.

"Cromwell, our chief of men, who through a cloud,
    Guided by faith and matchless fortitude,
    To peace and truth thy glorious way hast ploughed."
                                    —MILTON.

THE famous Navigation Act, which brought on the war between England and Holland, was one of the last acts in the life of the great Englishman Oliver Cromwell. Before telling the stories of the fine old Sea Admirals who fought in that war for the power of the seas, let us see what this man Cromwell had already done for his country.

Oliver Cromwell was a very giant among men, the "wonder of Europe and the glory of his age." Like the Pilgrim Fathers, he was a Puritan, steeped in the language of his Bible, intolerant of Roman Catholics. He had a mighty brain and a great soul; but he was no perfect hero, no spotless saint. He was just a strong man, who did what he thought best for his country in a difficult age.

The young Oliver was four years old when

Queen Elizabeth died and James became King of England. There is a story that, when he was a small baby, a large monkey seized him out of his cradle and carried him up on to the roof of the house. Another story says, that the very year of James's accession, his little son, Prince Charles, was worsted at "fisticuffs" while playing with Oliver Cromwell, who was but a year older than himself. But as the little Prince did not speak till he was five, and crawled on his hands and knees till he was seven, this is not likely.

It was a sorry day for England when this same young prince became king, on the death of his father in 1625, and the long quarrels were begun which ended only with his execution.

Now, England was governed by a king and Parliament. This latter consisted of a number of men from all parts of the country who decided on laws and taxes for the good of the land. In this Parliament sat young Oliver Cromwell. No one thought much of him. He slouched in and out in a home-spun suit, took little part publicly, and seemed glad enough to return to his farm, his wife and children, near Ely, in the eastern counties. It was not till Charles had plunged his country into civil war, by reason of his unjust taxation, that Cromwell rose to play his great part.

There was no standing army in England at this time. Troops were raised by private people, and Oliver Cromwell found himself in command of a troop of horse. Together with his parliamentary friends he was present at the first battle against the king. The king, helped by his fiery nephew, Prince Rupert, fresh over from the Thirty Years' War, was victorious. Cromwell knew why.

"Your troops," he said to one of his friends, "are old decayed serving-men, and the king's troops are gentlemen's sons. Do you think that the spirits of such base and mean fellows will ever be able to encounter gentlemen, that have honour and courage and resolution in them?"

The final result of the whole war lay in these words. Cromwell now chose men for the army who were sternly Puritan, who had their hearts in the cause, who had some conscience in what they did. Every soldier henceforth had to undergo a severe training. Cromwell himself, having learned from a Dutchman the art of war, drilled the men, until he had a cavalry regiment under his orders so fiery with zeal, so well restrained, that no body of horse could compare with it. No longer was there any thought of flight, none of retreat; deeds of eternal fame were done, endless and infinite. "From that day forward they were never beaten." So Cromwell and his Ironsides, as the soldiers were called, advanced to victory. Red coats were worn for the first time in this "New Model Army," as it was called.

The king was finally beaten and brought to trial in London. Then came the signing of the death-warrant by Cromwell and fifty-seven others, and preparations for the execution. The dignity which had failed the poor king in his life, came to him in these last days. He was allowed to say good-bye to his young children, a scene among the most pathetic in history. Having taken them on his knee and kissed them again and yet again, he ordered them to be taken away. When they reached the door they flew back to his arms, sobbing aloud, until the wretched King Charles tore himself away, only to fall on his knees in prayer.

Firmly he mounted the scaffold. As his head was lifted up to the sight of his subjects, a groan of pity and horror burst from the crowd. The news was received throughout Europe in silent horror.

But the death of the king was a great landmark in history. The old rule was behind, the new rule was before. A new life had arisen for England, which would affect the history of Europe.

Oliver Cromwell was now a king in all but name. Of his campaigns in Ireland and Scotland there is no time to tell. At the age of forty-three he had girt on his sword. At the age of fifty-two he laid it down.

"See what a multitude of people come to attend your triumph," they said to him when he returned from the wars.

"More would come to see me hanged," he had answered with a careless smile, knowing how unpopular he was.

·The country had been torn by war for ten years. Cromwell now turned his attention to a settlement of affairs. And first and foremost came the Act giving to the English increased power at sea, with more far-reaching results than even Oliver Cromwell could foresee.

36. TWO FAMOUS ADMIRALS.

"And sweep through the deep
While the stormy winds do blow,
While the battle rages long and loud,
And the stormy winds do blow."
—CAMPBELL.

CROMWELL had conquered all upon the land. He now turned to the sea, and tried to improve the trade of England by stopping the Dutch ships from bringing so much goods to English shores. No longer now could Dutch ships carry corn from Russia to England; no longer could they fish so freely for herrings off the English coast to take to Germany and other countries. No longer could they be the chief carriers of Europe, "waggoners of the sea." The ships of England were to take their own share of the world's sea-traffic.

From olden days England had claimed her right over the English Channel.

"It is the custom of the English to command at sea," the king used to say with pride. Indeed up to this time the flags of all other countries had been lowered before the flag of England while sailing through the narrow English Channel.

One day—it was in the year 1651—a Dutch fleet passed through the Channel without lowering the flag in salute to an English ship which it passed. The English admiral asked the reason of this insult, and as the Dutch captain refused to explain, he captured the flagship.

Relations now became very strained between the two countries. War was not yet declared, when suddenly one day the Dutch admiral, Tromp, sailed into the English Channel and anchored off the south coast with forty ships.

Now this Admiral Tromp was a great man. He had been born at Brille, the Beggars' town, and had gone to sea as a very little boy. At the age of eleven he had seen his father murdered on board his ship by English sea-robbers. Later in life the brave sailor Piet Hein, who had taken the Silver Fleet, was shot at his side. So Martin Tromp had seen a good deal of life and service, and he was one of Holland's greatest admirals.

But Tromp had his equal in the English admiral, Blake. Both men had been born in the same year; but while Tromp had gone to sea as a very small boy, Blake had not begun his seafaring career till he was fifty. In those days it was not thought necessary that an admiral or a captain should be a sailor. One man was in command of the soldiers on board the ship, another in command of the sailors and the ship herself. There was no uniform such as seamen have to-day. Each man dressed as he liked. Now, as Blake had fought well on land, he was put in command of a fleet of ships. He was cruising about in the English Channel one summer afternoon in 1652. One story says that he was sitting in his cabin with his officers, their swords lying on the table before them, when the windows of the ship were suddenly shattered.

"It is very ill-bred of Tromp to break my windows," said Blake, knowing that the Dutch admiral was not far off.

Then crash came the Dutch flagship into the English one; guns boomed over the quiet sea. For five long hours the fleets fought fiercely under Tromp and Blake, and the sun had long since set when, disabled and shattered, the Dutch ships sailed away for Holland, and Blake made his way to Dover to make known to Cromwell what had happened.

War now blazed out between the two countries —war for the command of the sea. It was just a year after their first fight when Blake and Tromp met again. The Dutch admiral, with some eighty ships and ten fireships, was sailing about midway between the English and Dutch coasts when he met Blake. But Blake, with forty ships, was totally unprepared to encounter such a superior force as now lay before him on the sea. He hastily called his officers together and they resolved to fight, though at such a disadvantage. But Tromp and his splendid fleet was too strong for them. The Dutch gained the victory, and in triumph Tromp tied a broom to his mast-head and sailed down the Channel, boasting that he would sweep the sea of every English ship! A few months later a more equal fight took place, and this time Blake was triumphant. The war had resolved itself into a duel between these two famous admirals. Now one was victorious, now the other.

In a later fight Blake was severely wounded, and the " Sea King," as the English called him, was unable to fight any longer. Soon after this, Martin Tromp, the " father of sailors," was killed.

" I am done for. Maintain the battle, my children," he gasped, as he fell mortally wounded on the deck of his ship.

When the news of the admiral's death spread through the fleets, as if by common consent, all stopped firing. A great man had died, and the fleets each sailed away in silence.

Both countries grew tired of the conflict, and were glad enough to make peace in the year 1654. True, the Dutch had to consent to the old tribute to the English flag; but they were still supreme on the seas, and though England was learning much from them, though she was growing stronger every day, yet at this time there was no Power in Europe which could compete with Holland on the high seas.

37. DE RUYTER.

"Henceforth must all your fleets be free
On every coast from east to west."
—Vondel.

The war with England was over. It had lasted two years, and Holland had suffered deeply, more even than in her eighty years of war with Spain; for during the war all trade had stopped, 1000 ships had been lost, and Admiral Tromp was dead.

Tromp was dead, but an abler man than Tromp had come forward during the war, and was now to save his country and make himself a name of undying fame. Michiel de Ruyter was born at Flushing in the year 1607. His grandfather was a trooper, and therefore called De Ruyter, "the rider." His boyhood was passed at Flushing. Here he could look out over the sea, where the Dutch ships returned laden with the wealth of the Indies. He would hear wondrous stories of adventure, until his eager mind grew restless. He was never much of a scholar.

There is a story told of him at ten years of age. Some workmen were repairing the steeple of Flushing, and young De Ruyter thought he would climb the scaffolding and mount the ladder, by which he could reach the dizzy pinnacle at the top. He arrived safely, but while he was perched at the very top the workmen removed the ladder, and nothing was left the boy but to slide down the steep pinnacle as best he might. Looking up, the burghers of the town saw a little figure waving his cap fearlessly from the top and then prepare for his perilous descent. With his nail-shod boots he kicked away a slate and placed his little foot on the wooden bar below the slate, then the other foot kicked away another, till slate after slate crashed into the street below, and the boy moved slowly downwards. At last he reached the scaffold and soon appeared in the street below.

Courage, cool-headedness, and resource,— these were to make a man out of the fearless boy. He was now apprenticed to a ropemaker at 1d. a-day; but as he was longing to be at sea, to sea he went at the age of eleven. At the age of fifteen he was fighting on shore with other Dutch sailors against Spain. His courage marked him out above his comrades, and when he was taken prisoner on the Spanish coast, he escaped and walked all the way home through Spain, France, and Belgium.

When war broke out with England, De Ruyter was given some ships and fought under Tromp with marked success. It was therefore to this man that Holland looked when war broke out again between the two countries in 1666.

Much had happened since the last war. The great English admiral, Blake, was dead. He had died on the sea, within sight of the home for which he had been yearning, just a year before the death of his master, Oliver Cromwell. An event of the greatest importance had taken place two years later, when Charles II. ascended the English throne and England had a king once more. The son of Charles I. had lived a great part of his life as an exile in Holland, and now, when he was called upon to return to England, he was given a magnificent feast at Amsterdam.

"My love for you is as great as that of all the other kings put together," he told the Dutch people when he left their hospitable shores.

He left his sister Mary amongst them, with her young son, William of Orange, and no one could foresee that a short four years was to make Charles II. the most active enemy of Holland.

Now Charles had married a Portuguese princess, and she had brought him as part of her dowry the possession of a port on the coast of India called Bombay, a little to the north of the famous Goa [1] of Portuguese fame. This was not pleasing news for Holland, for it strengthened the English East India Company, and the Dutchmen trembled for their trade in the East.

Again Charles annoyed the Dutch by capturing their colony in America, New Amsterdam, as they had called it, after their own capital. The English renamed it New York, and New York is the largest

[1] See Book II. chapter 34.

city in America and the richest in the world to-day.
In the East and West, England was competing with
Holland on the seas, and war at last broke out
between the two countries. De Ruyter was now
made Admiral of Holland, and a splendid new
fleet was placed under his command.

"The eyes of all the world are upon us," he
cried to his officers and men. "Behave, then, as
honest and brave men, bearing yourselves as you
ought. We have no need to fear our enemies,
nor to despise them, because they are soldiers
and sailors. Be resolved, then, to conquer or to
die."

The most memorable sea-fight of modern days
was now to take place between the Dutch under
De Ruyter on the one side and the English under
Prince Rupert on the other. It began on June
11, 1666, and lasted for four days, till the English
ships were disabled, powder and shot were spent,
and they were obliged to retreat. Through a thick
sea-mist the ships made their way home after tho
four days' contest for the ocean, which has not
been equalled to this day.

"English sailors may be killed, but they cannot
be conquered," a great Dutch leader had said.
Holland had now proved as unconquerable as England herself. All Europe rang with praise of the
brave De Ruyter. The little cabin-boy of forty-
nine years ago had become one of the greatest men
of his time. Humbly enough he took his great

victory. "And De Ruyter gave thanks to God, then swept out his cabin and fed his fowls," says his historian.

A short time later the thunder of Dutch guns in the Thames awoke England to a sense of her weakness, and the great Dutch admiral, after burning ships in the river, sailed proudly along the English coast, master of the Channel.

38. THE FOUNDER OF PENNSYLVANIA.

"And they whose firm endurance gained
    The freedom of the souls of men,
Whose hands, unstained with blood, maintained
    The swordless commonwealth of Penn."
                                —WHITTIER.

Now, as in the reign of James I. of England the Pilgrim Fathers had sailed to America to escape persecution, so now under Charles II. another persecuted band of men turned their eyes towards a home beyond the Atlantic. These men were known as Friends or Quakers. They were very strict, and thought it wrong to serve as soldiers. The king wanted men to fight in his Dutch wars, but these men refused : so they were fined, imprisoned, and whipped. At last one of the Quaker leaders, William Penn, asked the king to give him some land in America, where he might take his band of Quakers, that they might live in peace on the far side of the great Atlantic. The king consented, and gave him a large tract of country in the neighbourhood of New York, which had just been taken from the Dutch.

" Let us call the new land Sylvania," said Penn, " on account of the woods abounding there."

" We will add the honoured name of Penn," said the king. So the country became Pennsylvania, by which name it is known to-day as one of the United States of America.

For this land Penn was to pay the king two beaver-skins a-year, as well as a fifth of all the gold and silver found in the country. An expedition was at once sent out to take formal possession of the new country, while Penn himself prepared to follow.

" You are our brothers," said the new settlers when the Indians appeared, " and we will live like brothers with you. There shall be one broad path for you and us to walk in."

William Penn left England on the last day of August 1682, with a hundred Quakers in the ship Welcome. Like the little Mayflower, sixty years before, the Welcome had a terrible time on the sea. Smallpox broke out and raged so fiercely that thirty emigrants died before the ship reached America. After a two months' voyage — a fast passage for those days — the Welcome arrived, and Penn landed on the banks of the Delaware river with his sadly thinned band. About 100 miles up the great river the beginnings of an infant city had already been marked out.   In an open boat Penn started up the river.   The scenery was wholly enchanting.   The thickly wooded shores shone with the red and golden tints of autumn, wildfowl abounded, and the charm of the new country must have impressed its owner not a little.   Penn was received joyfully by the Quaker party who had arrived before him, while the old Dutch and Swedish settlers were anxious to catch a glimpse of their new governor.

The building of the great city went gaily forward, while Penn arranged a great meeting with the Indians at a given spot on the shores of the Delaware river.   The natives arrived in great numbers, fully armed, and sat down in a circle under a spreading elm-tree, round a great fire. In the front were the chiefs and aged men, while behind were the young men, women, and children.   It was November now, and the autumn leaves had fallen to the ground.   As Penn drew near, unarmed, the Indians laid down their weapons of war and prepared to listen to him. A sky-blue sash distinguished the leader from his friends.   He began solemnly :—

"The great God who made you and me, who rules the heavens and the earth, knows that I and my friends have a hearty desire to live in peace and friendship with you, and serve you to the uttermost of our power.   It is not our custom to use hostile weapons against our fellow-creatures, so we have come unarmed. We wish not to do harm, but to do good."

Penn then unrolled the document he carried in his hands, and read aloud the treaty to which he wanted them to agree.

All William Penn's Christians and all Indians should be brothers, as the children of one Father, joined together in head and heart. All paths should be open and free to both Christians and Indians. All Indians should teach their children of this firm chain of friendship, that it might become stronger and stronger and be kept bright and clean, without rust or spot. And the Indians declared, "while the rivers and creeks should run, while the sun, moon, and stars should endure," they would live in peace with the English.

In token of this Penn called the new city Philadelphia, the city of brotherly love. It grew very rapidly. Hardly a month passed that did not bring shiploads of emigrants, attracted thither by Penn's great humanity and his peaceful relations with the Indians.

Having made a success of his colony, Penn returned to England, where he died some time later. And the Indians of Pennsylvania, who had loved him as a brother, sent some beautiful skins to make a cloak for his widow, as they said, " to protect her while passing through the thorny wilderness without her guide."

Philadelphia to-day is one of the largest cities
in the United States.   The New City Hall, which
rises from her midst, is one of the highest buildings in the world, and it is surmounted by a colossal
figure of the founder of the great city of brotherly
love.

39. THE 'PILGRIM'S PROGRESS.'

"So I awoke, and behold it was a dream."—BUNYAN.

IN the very same year that Penn left England to
found the colony of Pennsylvania, a book was finding its way into all parts of Europe, and was fill-
ing men with wonder and delight.   The 'Pilgrim's
Progress' was written in English, and was soon
translated into Dutch and sent over the seas to
the Dutch and English colonies in America.   Soon
after it was translated into no less than eighty-
four different languages, and is to-day one of " the
most popular and most widely read of all English
books."

It was written in prison by John Bunyan, a
poor man, the son of a tinker.   For his religious
opinions he was thrown into prison at Bedford,
where he was kept for twelve years.   The Bible
was his constant companion, and the very language of his book is the language of the Bible
itself.   The story is the journey of a man called
Christian from his home, the City of Destruction,

to the Heavenly City, and the whole beautiful story has a deep meaning running through it.

"I dreamed, and behold I saw a man clothed in rags," begins Bunyan, "standing with his face from his home, with a book in his hand and a great burden upon his back."

This man was Christian, the hero of the story, and the burden was his sins.

"What shall I do?" he cried pitifully to his friends, for he was feeling the weight of his sins.

"Do you see yonder wicket - gate and yonder shining light?" said one, Evangelist, to him. "Keep that light in your eye and go up directly thereto; so shalt thou see the gate, at which, when thou knockest, it shall be told thee what thou shalt do."

So Christian started off, as Evangelist had suggested, with his burden on his back, to reach the Heavenly City. But soon he found himself struggling in a bog. The name of the bog was the Slough of Despond, and by reason of his load Christian began to sink in the mire. Then came a man called Help, who stretched forth his hand and drew him out. So Christian went on again. And now he met a man known as Mr Worldly Wiseman, who advised him to turn elsewhere to get rid of his burden. Christian was following his advice when Evangelist again met him.

"What dost thou here, Christian? Did I not

direct thee to the little wicket - gate ? " he said sorrowfully.

Ashamed of his weakness, Christian took the narrow path once more. At last he reached the wicket - gate. " Knock, and it shall be opened unto you," was written above. Christian knocked and passed through. He will know the road, for it is strait and narrow and the wrong road is wide. Then a wonderful thing happened. He came to a cross, and as he stood before it his burden rolled off his back. Three shining ones appeared, who stripped him of his rags, clothed him with a change of raiment, set a mark on his forehead, and gave him a sealed roll to give up at the gates of heaven.

He now passed on, meeting various friends on the way. Then they came to the Hill Difficulty. There were two roads at the foot, one marked Danger, the other Destruction. Though his friends took these roads and were never heard of again, Christian went straight up over the hill and reached the Palace Beautiful, built by the Lord of the Hill for strangers. Two lions guarded the way, and Christian paused.

" Is thy strength so small ? " cried the watch-man. " Fear not the lions, for they are chained. Keep in the midst of the path and no hurt shall come unto thee."

At the Palace Beautiful he was armed from head to foot by the ladies Prudence, Piety, and Charity, for he had yet to go through the Valley of the Shadow of Death. Two men appeared to him on the borders of it, warning him to go back, for it was dark and full of horrors. But Christian went through with it, to find the sun shining on the other side. Faithful, a pilgrim like himself, now joined him, and they went forward together. Together they came to Vanity Fair, which had been going on for five thousand years, and through which they must pass to reach the Heavenly City.

"What will you buy?" cried the noisy rough men who were selling there.

"We buy the truth," answered Christian and Faithful. A great hubbub broke forth, which ended in the death of Faithful, and Christian went on alone.

A man called Hopeful now joined him, and together they crossed the River of Life. But here they strayed into By - path Meadow, lost themselves in Doubting Castle, and were seized by Giant Despair. With a key called Promise Christian opened the door of their dungeon, and they went forward once more. And now they reached the Enchanted Ground, Doubting Castle could be seen no more, and between them and their last rest there only remained the deep river of Death, over which was no bridge. On the hill beyond glittered the towers and domes of the Heavenly City. The sun shone on the city, which was of pure gold. Through the deep waters of the

river went Christian and Hopeful. On the farther
bank two Shining Men were waiting to lead them
up the last hill to the city. There they were received with "ten thousand welcomes, with shouts
which made the very heavens echo, and with
trumpets."

"These pilgrims are come from the City of Destruction, for the love that they bear to the King
of this place," said the Shining Men.

So Christian and Hopeful were taken into the
presence of the King, and as they entered their
raiments shone like gold, crowns were placed on
their heads, harps were put in their hands, and the
bells in the city rang again for joy.

"So I awoke," says Bunyan, "and, behold, it was
a dream."

40. THE HOUSE OF ORANGE.

"Orange above, De Witt under;
Who says nay, strike him thunder."
                    —*Old Dutch Song*.

HOLLAND was now supreme on the seas, and she
stood high among the nations of Europe. Under
her leader, De Witt, she had thriven and pros-
pered. She was to prosper yet more under the
young Prince of Orange, who now comes on the
scene. Descended from that William the Silent
who had more than a hundred years before de-

livered his land from the yoke of Spain, he was
the ancestor of Holland's present queen. He was
to play a great part in preparing England for her
wondrous future.

When Charles I. had been torn from his weeping children to be beheaded, he had left a daughter
called Mary, who married a great-nephew of William the Silent and lived her life in Holland.
They had but one delicate child, born in 1650,
the little Prince William, over whose birth the
country rejoiced not a little. Always weak and
ailing, he was but ten years old when his widowed
mother went over to England to visit her brother,
Charles II., just restored to the throne. There she
caught the smallpox and died.

The little heir of the famous House of Orange
was now alone. Fatherless, motherless, almost
friendless, the boy was brought up by men who
looked on his very life as a danger to the State,
then under John de Witt. He was closely
guarded. At the age of fifteen the friends in
whom he had confided were removed, and he was
kept as a State prisoner in the great castle at
The Hague. With tears in his eyes the little
prince begged for friends with an energy that was
pitiful. The refusal affected his health. He was
racked with a cough, he could only breathe in
the purest air, he could only sleep when raised
on many pillows, his face was scored with lines
of ceaseless pain. Other boys might have perished,

but this boy only braced himself and learned his lesson of self-control. He learned to guard his speech, to keep secrets, to hide all passion under a coolness of manner which lasted through his life. Those who brought him good news saw no trace of pleasure in his face, those who saw him after defeat detected no shade of sorrow. But those who knew him well, knew that under this ice a fierce fire was burning; that where he loved, he loved with the whole force of his strong soul; that when death parted him from these, tears of agony overwhelmed him. He always spoke Dutch, but he knew English and German.

At the age of seventeen he showed a knowledge of the State that surprised older men. At eighteen he sat among the fathers of the States-General or Parliament. At twenty-one, on a "day of gloom and terror," he was placed at the head of his country. This was how it came about.

There was at this time a wonderful King of France called Louis XIV.[1] This king had set his heart on conquering Holland by land, while his friend Charles II. was fighting the Dutch by sea. So in the summer of 1672 he led his great French army across the Rhine and fell upon the Dutch. They were totally unprepared, and the French triumphantly swept through the country, carrying all before them. When the glare of the French watch-fires was seen from Amsterdam, De

[1] See Book III. chapter 44.

Witt made an heroic resolve. Holland had once been saved by the sea. She should be saved again. So the dykes were cut which protected the low-lying land from the sea, and soon the friendly water had flowed over the land and saved Holland from a foreign foe. Hundreds of houses and gardens were buried beneath the waves, peasants were flying before the invading French, when De Witt proposed peace. Then the people rose in anger, they thought that he wanted to sell their country to France, and they turned in their despair to the young Prince of Orange.

"Our Prince must be Stadtholder," they cried.

Then, forgetting all they owed to De Witt, they murdered him brutally at The Hague, and William, the young, silent Prince of Orange, became their head. Both England and France now begged him to submit to their terms of peace.

"Do you not see," said the English, "that your country is lost?"

"There is a sure way never to see it lost," answered William, "and that is to die in the last ditch."

So Holland was saved, and province after province was won back from France, by William's dauntless resolve.

The country was still struggling against the growing power of France when the Prince was laid low with smallpox. Devotedly nursed by a faithful friend, he fought his way back to life, while he made plans, in his quiet way, to stop the dangerous strength of Louis XIV. of France.

In 1675 he married Mary, his first cousin, niece of Charles II., reigning King of England, and herself heiress to the throne.

Thus peace was secured, and events hurried on to that fateful day when William and Mary should be crowned King and Queen of England.

41. WILLIAM'S INVITATION.

> "Calm as an under-current, strong to draw
> Millions of waves into itself and run
> From sea to sea, impervious to the sun
> And ploughing storm, the spirit of Nassau
> Swerves not."
> —WORDSWORTH, *William III.*

WILLIAM and Mary were living peaceably at The Hague when Charles II. died in 1685, leaving no children. He was succeeded by his brother James, a Roman Catholic. The next heir to the English throne was Mary, William's wife. England was considering the matter of succession when a son was born to James, an unfortunate little prince, destined to seventy-seven years of wandering and exile, and known to history as the Old Pretender. His birth brought matters to a crisis. He was sure to be brought up as a Roman Catholic like his father, and England wanted a Protestant ruler.

So an invitation was written and secretly con-
veyed to The Hague begging William to come
over to England with an army and restore the
Protestant religion. The Prince of Orange accepted
the invitation. Though he must fight against his
own father-in-law, there were larger questions at
stake than mere family ties. A camp was formed
at once. Soldiers and sailors were raised. The
gunmakers of Utrecht worked at pistols and
muskets by day and night, the saddlers at Amsterdam toiled at harness, the docks were busy with
shipping. And ever and anon a light swift skiff
sped between the Dutch and English coasts. It
was an anxious time. The Prince maintained an
icy calmness, but to his friend he wrote openly:
" My sufferings, my disquiet, are dreadful. I hardly
see my way. Never in my life did I feel so much
the need of God's guidance."

By the autumn of 1688 all was ready. He said
good-bye to the States-General, alone standing calm
amid his weeping friends.

"I am now leaving you, perhaps never to return," he told them. "If I should fall in defence
of my religion, take care of my beloved wife."

Though beaten back on his first venture by a
violent storm, William set sail with his 600 ships,
accompanied by fifty men-of-war, for the shores
of England. As the Dutch fleet passed the narrow
Straits of Dover the flourish of trumpets, the clash
of cymbals, and the rolling of the drums was heard

on either shore. As night drew on the watchers on the southern coast beheld the sea in a blaze of light, through which three huge lanterns flamed from the leading ship, which bore to England William, Prince of Orange.

Meanwhile the news that his son-in-law had landed at Torbay reached James, who was already preparing to oppose him. He had a splendid army, but he could not depend on his men. Soon they began to desert him and flock to the standard of William, until at last he fled to London in despair, only to hear that his daughter Anne had fled secretly.

"God help me!" cried the wretched king, "for my own children have forsaken me."

His spirit was broken now. Nothing was left him but flight. He arranged for the safety of his wife and child, declaring he himself would stick to his post. It was a December night. The king and queen went to bed as usual. When all was quiet James called to his side a faithful French friend to whom he had confided his secret.

"I confide to you my queen and my son. You must risk everything to carry them to France," he said.

It was a bitter night in December. Wrapping his own cloak round the ill-fated baby of seven months old, and giving his hand to the weeping queen, the Frenchman took them down the backstairs and placed them in an open boat on the Thames. The rain was falling in torrents, the wind roared, the water was rough, but the little party of fugitives escaped to a ship and set sail with a fair wind for France.

The next day the king rose at three in the morning, and taking the Great Seal of State, he disappeared down a secret passage, crossed the Thames, and flinging the Great Seal into the midst of the stream, he attempted to follow his wife and child to France. He was captured and brought back to London ; but William had no wish to have his royal father-in-law on his hands, and James, the fugitive king, was allowed to embark for France.

Then, amid the peal of bells, the blast of trumpets, and the joyous shouts of the citizens, William and Mary were proclaimed King and Queen of England.

The great Revolution was over.

But James had no intention of giving up his kingdom so quietly. By the help of Louis XIV. he raised an army and sailed over to assert his rights in Ireland.

42. THE STRUGGLE IN IRELAND.

"Down thy valleys, Ireland, Ireland,
Down thy valleys green and sad,
Still thy spirit wanders wailing,
Wanders wailing, wanders mad."
—NEWBOLT.

WILLIAM now turned his attention to Ireland, where James II. was stirring up the country against him. Neither was he the first English ruler to turn his eyes towards that unhappy land —that beautiful "Emerald Isle" across the seas, ever in a state of unrest and misery.

What was the story of this strange, lonely island, which was so close to England and yet so far?

Ireland, or Erin, as the poets love to call her, has been compared to a lovely and lonely bride whom England has wedded but has never won. But the time must come—perhaps is not far distant — when bridegroom and bride shall understand one another and shall go forward hand in hand—

"Strong with a strength that no fate might dissever,
One with a oneness no force could divide."

Oliver Cromwell had ruled the people with a firm hand. Indeed he alone of English rulers stamped his image on the country. For eight weary years the Irish had fought for Charles I., and on his death they proclaimed his son king. This had roused Cromwell to action. In the summer of 1649 he landed in Ireland with a huge army. The following spring he returned to England, leaving Ireland once more crushed and lifeless. Her Parliament had ceased to exist, a few Protestant members were transferred to London. Vast military colonies were established by Cromwell, and the large Roman Catholic landowners were exiled to a corner of the country between the Shannon and the sea, called Connaught.

To all outward appearance England and Ireland were now one. But when the English people rose against James II., and drove him over to France, the people of Ireland, ever true to the Stuart cause and the Roman Catholic religion, resolved to support him. Here is one of the legends of how the king arrived in Ireland.

Erin lay awake in bed. Outside a storm was raging and rain was falling in torrents. The wind was howling and roaring down the chimney. Suddenly there was a tap at the door.

"Who is there?" asked Erin.

"It is I, James, son of Charles. I have been driven forth by robbers from the home of my ancestors. Give me shelter, I pray thee, from the fury of the storm."

Quickly Erin unbarred the door and brought in the hapless stranger. She took off his dripping cloak, gave him dry clothes, put fresh peat upon the fire, supplied him with food and shelter, and promised to help him.

The appearance of James in Ireland was hailed with enthusiasm. As a king, as a Roman Catholic, as a man in deep misfortune, he had a claim on the feelings of a warm-hearted race of people. He had landed at Kinsale on March 12, 1689. From Cork to Dublin people ran before him in crowds to greet him with tears and blessings.

But the Irish, with the hapless exile James at their head, were no match for the great military force now landing in the north, commanded in person by William III. of England.

" The country is worth fighting for," said William to his mixed army of English and Dutch as he marched through Ireland for the first time in his life.

He noted the rich greenness of the land, the bays and rivers so admirably fitted for trade. Where were the forests of masts that lay in every harbour of his native Holland ? Where the warehouses that should have lined the quay ? Could he not give these people the government and religion that had made Holland the wonder of the world ?

He marched on till he came to the green banks of the river Boyne. As the glorious beauties of the valley burst upon him he could not suppress his admiration. Here on the neighbouring hill of Dromore was the camp of James II. Here was to be fought one of the most famous battles of the age.

An old story says, that as the exiled king stood looking over the fair country, his crown fell from his head and rolled down the steep green slope till it plunged into the dark still waters below. On the walls of Drogheda, at the mouth of the Boyne, waved the flags of James and Louis XIV., side by side : every soldier, Irish and French, had a white badge in his hat.

William's keen eye took in the whole situation.

"I am glad to see you, gentlemen," he said ; "if you escape me now, the fault will be mine."

"Their army is but small," said one of his Dutch officers.

"They may be stronger than they look," answered William, for he knew that many Irish regiments were hidden from view.

The 1st of July dawned. The sun rose bright and cloudless. With drums beating, William and his army advanced to the banks of the Boyne. Each man had bound a green bough in his hat. Ten abreast, the soldiers then plunged into the stream, until the Boyne seemed to be alive with muskets and waving boughs. It was not till they had reached the middle that they realised their danger. Whole regiments of foot and horse, hidden from their sight, now seemed to start out of the very earth. A wild shout rose from the opposite shore, as the Irish and French together rushed to battle. But the great army led by William was too much for them. The Irish foot-soldiers were untrained, badly armed, and unused to action. True, the cavalry stood firm, but their valour was powerless to win the day. At the first shock of reverse James fled to Dublin. He arrived convulsed with rage.

"Madam," he cried to the wife of one of his brave officers—"Madam, your countrymen have run away."

"If they have, sire," answered the Irish lady with ready wit, "your majesty seems to have won the race."

And the old stories say that James never stopped running till he reached the coast, when he took ship for France!

43. THE SIEGE OF VIENNA BY THE TURKS.

"Think with what passionate delight
The tale was told in Christian halls
How Sobieski turned to flight
The Moslem from Vienna's walls."
—Lord Houghton.

Among the great names that fill the stage of Europe in the last quarter of the seventeenth century — William III., King of England and Holland; Louis XIV., King of France; Peter the Great, Tsar of Russia; and Charles XII. of Sweden — the name of John Sobieski, King of Poland,

must not be forgotten. Sobieski was a national
hero rather than a great king. He might well
have belonged to the old crusading[1] days, for his
head, even now, was full of crusading ideas. With
other Christian rulers he watched the growth of
Mohammedanism over Western Europe with in-
creasing anxiety.

For the last two hundred years the Ottoman
empire had stood high among the Powers of
Europe. Greece was subject to Turkey; parts of
Hungary, Austria, and Russia owned her sway.
Now in the year 1683 the Turks were marching
on Austria's capital, Vienna, and Vienna was totally
unprepared for a siege. The Emperor of Austria
was no soldier, so he removed his court to a place
some fifteen miles away and calmly awaited events.
The Viennese now turned to Sobieski, the King
of Poland, a well-known champion of the Christians,
a well-known hater of the Turks. The fate of
Austria hung on his reply. To Sobieski the appeal
had all the old romance of the Crusades.

"Yes," he answered in haste, "I will come and
help you."

And "flinging his powerful frame into the saddle
and his great soul into the cause," the King of
Poland began eagerly to recruit his scattered army.
Meanwhile the defence of the city was intrusted
to Count Stahremberg. He instantly set all hands
to work.

---

[1] See Book II. chapter 18.

"Set fire to the suburbs," he ordered. "They shall not serve as cover to the enemy."

The flames rose high around the city, a wind sprang up, and Vienna herself had a narrow escape of being burned to the ground. Presently the main force of the enemy appeared on the plain in front of Vienna. In a short time thousands of Turkish tents had sprung up, and the camp was alive with bustle and excitement. The tents of the Grand Vizier, or Prime Minister, were conspicuous with their green silk worked in gold and silver, their pearls and precious stones, their gorgeous Eastern carpets. Around them were arranged baths, fountains, flower-gardens, and even a menagerie of animals. From time to time the Grand Vizier, in gorgeously embroidered robes, was carried out in a litter to inspect the works.

The siege had begun in real earnest. Assault followed assault. Day by day Stahremberg climbed up the lofty fretted spire of the cathedral church in the heart of Vienna; he looked gloomily over the busy Turkish camp and owned sadly to himself that the Turks were gaining ground inch by inch. Sickness and famine followed, and still Sobieski did not come.

Sobieski had left Poland a few days after the siege had begun in July, but the way was long; he himself was stout and heavy. It was the end of August before he reached the outskirts of Vienna. Here he found a little crowd of German princes awaiting him, together with Duke Charles of Lorraine, ancestor of the Imperial House of Austria. Here was the Hanoverian prince, afterwards George I. of England; here was Eugene of Savoy, the colleague of Marlborough [1] at Blenheim; here were men who had fought in the battle of the Boyne, veterans of the Thirty Years' War,—all united in a common cause.

"We have not come to save a single city, but the whole of Christendom," said John Sobieski, as preparations for an attack on the Turks went forward.

Marching to within four miles of Vienna, the Christian army occupied the heights of the Kahlenberg.

The sun was just setting on the evening of September 11 when Sobieski and his generals stood on the crest of the hill. They could hear the Turkish cannonade raging vigorously, they could hear the feeble reply from the despairing garrison within the town. But Sobieski's rockets from the Kahlenberg brought new hope to the brave defenders, and Stahremberg despatched a messenger with a few urgent words : "No time to be lost! —no time indeed to be lost!"

Morning dawned misty and hot. The fate of Vienna depended on the events of the day. The army of the Christians began with a solemn service in the little chapel on the heights of the Kahlen-

[1] See Book III. chapter 47.

BK. III.   M

berg. Then a standard with a white cross on a red ground was unfurled amid shouts of enthusiasm, and the leaders of the great army moved forward. The sky-blue doublet of John Sobieski marked him out above his fellows, as the descent of the wooded slopes towards Vienna began.

The Grand Vizier's preparations for the battle were somewhat different. He slaughtered thirty thousand captives in cold blood and then ordered the advance.

Down the slopes poured the Christian army like a whirlwind, while the shout, " Long live Sobieski!" rolled along the lines. With all their faults the Turks did not know cowardice ; they fought as brave men, but they could not withstand the rush of the Christian army.

" Can you not help me ? " cried the Vizier in despair to one of his pashas.

" No," was the answer. " I know the King of Poland. It is impossible to resist him. Think only of flight."

Panic-stricken, the Turks fled, away through the wasted suburbs of Vienna, towards the frontier of Hungary. The Grand Vizier, weeping and cursing by turns, was hurried along with the stream.

By evening communication with Vienna was established, and Stahremberg led forth his starving garrison to greet his deliverers. Amid the shouts of the people John Sobieski entered Vienna, the city which he had saved from the Turks.

"How will the Emperor receive him?" the people asked in their joy; "for he has saved the empire."

They might well question. The Emperor received the deliverer of his people with a few cold words in Latin, for he was jealous of Sobieski's success. The King of Poland saw how matters stood. With a courteous chivalry that might have belonged to the middle ages, he saluted the Austrian emperor.

"I am happy, sire, to have been able to render you this slight service," he said simply.

A general chorus of admiration and thanksgiving arose from Europe. John Sobieski had not only saved Austria's capital, but he had destroyed the growing power of Turkey and forced the Mohammedans back to their own dominions.

44. THE GREATNESS OF FRANCE.

"L'État, c'est moi" (I am the State).
—Louis XIV.

Now, there was one man who watched the growing power of William of Orange with intense alarm. That man was Louis XIV. of France, who was now sheltering the unfortunate James. He had inherited a prosperous kingdom from his father, Louis XIII., and he had dreams of making an empire that should rival that of Charlemagne in

size and magnificence—dreams of a great Roman
Catholic union of which he himself should be the
head. He was but four and a half years old when
his father lay dying.

"I have been named Louis XIV.," the child
told the sinking king.

"Not yet, not yet," whispered his father, who
still clung to life.

But within a month the little Louis was indeed
King of France. Sitting in the carriage beside his
widowed mother, he entered the capital amid great
enthusiasm. Seated upon his throne, he received
the great men of the kingdom. Simply dressed
in a little velvet frock, he even stood up and made
them a speech, prompted by his governess.

Until he came of age, though king in name,
a great Minister, Mazarin, ruled the country for
him. He was a great statesman, and greatly increased the influence of France abroad. On the
death of Mazarin in 1661 Louis stepped firmly on
to the scene himself. He had grown up with the
hopeless idea that the king was supreme, that he
could rule as he liked, without the people, without
the Parliament.

"I am the State," he asserted firmly. "The king
alone rules, everything must centre in the king."
He made the same fatal mistake that had brought
the Stuart kings to grief in England. He tried
to rule alone, without the people.

Louis now set to work to make his Court the

most magnificent in Europe. Thither flocked
poets and play-writers, men of letters and great
ministers. And it was such as these that helped
to make France so great at this time.

Perhaps most important of all those at Louis'
Court was Colbert, the great Minister of Finance,
who raised France to take such a high place among
the commercial nations of his day. He invited
over the best workmen from other countries and
started manufactories of steel, iron, glass, and
tapestry. He built ships until France had a navy
strong enough to beat the combined fleets of England and Holland. He looked after the French
colonies in America and the West Indies. And
so he made the country richer and richer. No
longer did the ladies of Paris ride through the
dirty streets on mules, they had now carriages
and stage-coaches to convey them from place to
place.

There was Molière, the son of an upholsterer,
whose masterpieces of comedy so delighted the
king that he raised him to a high position of
wealth at the Court. There was Racine, who loved
to write of the old Greeks and Romans. There
was Pascal, whose beautiful 'Thoughts' made him
known as the "Plato of modern France." There
was La Fontaine, who wrote fables after the style
of the old Greek Æsop, which delight every French
child of to-day just as they delighted the children
of the seventeenth century. Then there was

Fénelon, scholar and man of letters, selected by the king to be tutor to his little grandson Louis.

Fénelon had come to the Court when little Louis was but seven years old. He was a wayward, self-willed child, who, like his grandfather the king, thought that everything must give way to his whims and wishes. Fénelon's task was no easy one, but gently and firmly he accomplished it, until the boy's wondering mind grasped the teaching of his high-souled tutor. He began to learn that there were higher things in life than the mere grandeur of kingship—that honour and courage were above all necessary, that religion must be real and very true. The boy loved the man who taught him of these things with a faithful love that stood the tests of time and exile.

"With you I am only little Louis," he would cry when he escaped from the pomps and shams of the French Court to the tutor, who, if he chided him, loved him as his very life. For this little Louis, Fénelon wrote stories and fables to illustrate the dangers of kingship. He called them the 'Adventures of Telemachus,' because he wrote them in the style of Homer's Odyssey. He wrote about an ideal king, who lived for his people and his country only and not for himself. But in course of time the stories got into the hands of the king himself. He was very angry, and Fénelon was ever after this in deep disgrace.

The wars of Louis XIV. also raised the fame of

Louis XIV. at Versailles.

France abroad. The French armies were better
equipped and disciplined than any others of that
age. The French wars with the Netherlands have
already been described. Louis' career of conquest
was only stayed by the Triple Alliance, made by
England, Holland, and Sweden. He extended the
frontiers of France in Alsace, and together with
his famous commanders, Condé and Turenne, he
conquered town after town in Germany.

All Europe feared him. He had taught his own
people to admire him by reason of his military
glory and skilful management. He was an absolute
despot. He held no Parliament, he raised taxes at
pleasure ; even the courts of justice yielded to the
absolute sway of the king, who interrupted the
ordinary course of the law as he pleased.

He built for himself a magnificent palace at
Versailles, eleven miles from Paris. He spent vast
sums of money, wrung from his people, upon gilded
halls and painted rooms, "magnificent but uncom-
fortable." It was a centre of pleasure and luxury,
built to the glory of one man, Louis XIV.

45. THE STORY OF THE HUGUENOTS.

"Thou Rochelle, our own Rochelle, proud city of the waters."
—MACAULAY.

No sooner was Colbert dead than Louis struck
a tremendous blow at the large Huguenot com-

munity in his kingdom. The massacre of St Bartholomew,[1] over 111 years before, had thinned their ranks; but a famous Act, known to history as the Edict of Nantes, had secured to them their rights as citizens of France. By this they could enjoy perfect freedom, they could hold offices side by side with Roman Catholics, they could build their own churches, teach in their own schools. So they had increased in numbers and in strength.

But in the year 1626, when Louis XIII. was reigning, their liberty was again threatened; they rose in revolt, and were besieged in their old stronghold—La Rochelle. The city was built in a crescent shape, round a fine land-locked bay, with a splendid harbour. It was sheltered from Atlantic storms by an island at the mouth of the harbour. So strong was the situation of La Rochelle, that the king, Louis XIII., and his great Minister Richelieu, had to bring the whole strength of the army to bear upon it. But stout Huguenot hearts beat within.

"We will not submit while there is one man left to shut the gates against the enemy," they said within the city walls.

Richelieu was determined to take the place. He built immense stone dykes out into the sea, across the harbour bar, from shore to shore. Where the water was too deep in the middle he filled huge ships with stones and sank them across the

[1] See Book III. chapter 11.

harbour mouth. It was a gigantic task, but it proved successful at last. Starvation began to tell on the heroic Huguenots, who could get no relief from without. Men, women, and children dropped dead in the streets, and after a resistance of fourteen months the city fell. And Richelieu, beside his king, rode into the death-stricken town of La Rochelle at the head of the royal army.

The Huguenots had again increased until they formed the most flourishing members of French trade. But Louis XIV. thought more about his own fame and power than of his country, and he now sought to convert or persecute them more fiercely than before. They were treated more and more harshly, until at length every career seemed closed to them. From time to time the king's messengers broke into their churches, placed their Bibles and hymn-books in a great pile, and set fire to them. Those that rebelled were hanged.

Then the king played his last card. In 1685 he revoked the famous Edict of Nantes, and thus struck the death-knell of the French Huguenots. With levers and pickaxes the Huguenot churches were knocked down. Children were torn from their mothers' arms to be brought up in the Roman Catholic faith, women were dragged from their sick-beds, hundreds were condemned to die, others were imprisoned for life.

"If God preserve the king, there will not be

one Huguenot left twenty years hence," said one
of Louis' friends.

Crushed, tormented, persecuted, there was nothing left them but flight, and even this was refused
to most of them. They must become Roman
Catholics or die. The frontiers of France were
strongly guarded, the coasts were watched. In
their desperate state the unhappy Huguenots
crossed the frontier, through forests, over trackless wastes, or by high mountain paths, where
no guard was stationed.

Numbers escaped into Switzerland, Germany,
and Holland. They mostly travelled under cover
of darkness in small parties. They disguised themselves in all sorts of ways. Some went as pedlars,
others as soldiers, huntsmen, beggars, or servants.
One well-known officer and his wife escaped to Holland dressed as orange - sellers, leading a donkey
with panniers. Two little children were carried
off in baskets slung across the back of a mule as
luggage. One lady of high birth escaped as a
peasant, with her infant son slung in a shawl at
her back, passed through the guards, and made
her way to London. Young girls browned their
faces and pushed wheelbarrows to escape detection.
Many hid in empty casks, and were thus carried
on board ships bound for England. Their sufferings were terrible. Numbers were caught and
brought back. Men and boys were put to serve
as galley-slaves in the vessels of war which sailed

up and down the Mediterranean Sea, five being chained to each oar.

Just a few were saved. The first admiral in France was a Huguenot. The king sent for him and begged him to become a Roman Catholic; but the old hero pointed to his grey hairs.

"For sixty years, sire, have I rendered to Cæsar the things which are Cæsar's: suffer me still to render unto God the things that are God's."

He was eighty years old, he had served his country well, and Louis spared him. But the great stream of Huguenot emigrants had left their country. It was the deathblow to several great branches of industry encouraged by Colbert. The silk manufacturers went over to London in a body. Amsterdam was filled with industrious French workers; Germany, Switzerland, all gained by the exodus. French ships were left unmanned, and the Huguenot seamen carried the news of their country's madness to the ends of the earth. Numbers sailed over the sea to America. A large party went to the Cape of Good Hope and joined the Dutch colony already thriving there under Van Riebeek.[1] Thus a blow was struck at the prosperity of France. Not only her industries, but the flower of her race was gone, exiled, banished to foreign lands.

The greatness of France had already begun to pass away.

[1] See Book III. chapter 34.

46. THE GREATEST GENERAL OF HIS AGE.

" Jack of Marlborough,
Who beat the Frenchman thorough and thorough."
—*Old English Rhyme.*

THOUGH the seventeenth century ended in peace, yet dark storm-clouds were hovering over Europe. Louis XIV. still reigned in France, William III. in England ; but it was towards distant Spain that the eyes of kings and people were now strained.

There on the throne of his forefathers sat a miserable and sickly king, whose death must end the long line of princes who had for two hundred years occupied the Spanish throne. The great question now engaging Europe was : Who should succeed him ? Spain had fallen from her high estate, but so vast still was the extent of her empire that under vigorous rule her old power might yet return. In 1700 the poor king died, leaving his kingdom to Philip, the young grandson of Louis XIV. of France, the younger brother of that little Louis loved and taught by Fénelon years before. Nothing could have been more pleasing to the ambition of Louis XIV. Gladly enough he despatched his grandson, a boy of seventeen, to the Court of Madrid, though the boy-king of Spain was in bitter tears at leaving his home in Paris for a long winter journey to his new kingdom.

"Remember there are no longer any Pyrenean mountains," were Louis' parting words to Philip.

Louis had promised faithfully never to unite the thrones of France and Spain, and it was with some uneasiness now that Europe watched him directing young Philip with a high hand.

No one felt more uneasy than William III. of England. His whole life had been a struggle to keep the ever-growing power of France within bounds. He distrusted Louis, and it was with reluctance that he acknowledged Philip as King of Spain. Now Louis went a step farther.

James, the exiled King of England, lay dying in France, when Louis entered his room and promised him to help his son Charles to regain the English throne when William should die. In a moment all England was in a blaze. The English people had never loved their Dutch king, but he had made them free, he had been the champion of the Protestant religion. Should the King of France dictate to them who was to be their king? A thousand times No. Rather would they fight. In the midst of these storms William was thrown one day from his horse and broke his collar-bone. In the wretched state of his health he had no strength to rally.

"There was a time when I should have been glad to have been delivered out of my difficulties,"

whispered the dying king to his lifelong Dutch
friend; "but I see another scene, and could wish
to live a little longer."

This was denied him. It was in the year 1702
that William died, leaving his sister-in-law Anne
to be Queen of England. Angrily the King of
France received the news of her accession, and
two months later war was declared by England
against France and Spain.

The command of the troops was given by Anne
to her old friend the Duke of Marlborough. This
was the man who was now to carry on the work
of his old master in baffling the ambitions of France
—the man who was to decide the fate of Europe.

Already glimpses of him have appeared from
time to time. He was one of those who deserted
his king to fight under the banner of William of
Orange. He had helped Anne to escape before
her father, James II., reached London. He had
later been caught plotting with the very king whom
he had deserted, and thrown into prison by William.
Pardoned and restored to favour, he became tutor
to Anne's little boy, heir to the throne; for Mary
had died of smallpox while still young, leaving no
child to succeed her and William.

Marlborough was ambitious and scheming, but
he was a marvellous soldier. He did not take up
his command till the age of fifty-two, an age when
the work of many men is nearly done; but he had
unbroken good fortune. Voltaire said that he

never besieged a fortress that he did not take, or
fight a battle that he did not win.

"Our Duke was as calm at the mouth of a
cannon as at the door of a drawing-room," said
one who served under him. "He was cold, calm,
resolute as fate."

"Yet those of the army who knew him best and
had suffered most from him admired him most of
all; and as he rode along the lines to battle, or
galloped up in the nick of time to a battalion
reeling from before the enemy's charge or shot,
the fainting men and officers got new courage as
they saw the splendid calm of his face, and felt
that his will made them irresistible."

Such was the Duke of Marlborough, the "greatest
general of his age."

47. THE BATTLE OF BLENHEIM.

> "'But everybody said,' quoth he,
> 'That 'twas a famous victory.'"
> —SOUTHEY.

AWAY in the heart of the German Black Forest
rises the river Danube, one of the largest rivers
in Europe. It is more than double the length of
the Rhine; it is swifter than the Seine. After
leaving Germany it waters the plains of Hungary,
supplies Vienna, the capital of Austria, and flows
into the Black Sea. But to-day we are only con-

cerned with a little village on the banks of this great river—the village of Blenheim, where the fate of Europe was to be decided by the Duke of Marlborough.

He had left Harwich in the April of 1704 and reached The Hague two days later. Heart-broken at the death from smallpox of her only son, the Duchess of Marlborough wanted to go with him. But "I am going into Germany," the Duke wrote to her from Holland, "where it would be impossible for you to follow me; but love me as you do now and no hurt can come to me."

Marlborough had no easy task before him. Louis XIV. had been victorious in Germany, and the French boundaries seemed growing larger and larger. He now had designs on Vienna, where he thought to decide the fate of the empire. This master-stroke of Louis roused Marlborough to a master-stroke in return, but he kept his plans a secret. Having completed his preparations at The Hague, he sailed round to Utrecht. All Europe was now watching his progress with the greatest interest and anxiety. With a huge army of English and Dutch soldiers he now marched southwards, his plans yet a secret from the world.

"I am in a house that has a view over the finest country that is possible to be seen," he wrote to his wife. "I see out of my chamber window the Rhine and the Neckar. I hope in eight days to meet with Prince Eugene."

Now, Prince Eugene of Savoy ruled over a little State bordering on France, and he had promised to help England against the growing power of Louis. The two generals now met for the first time, and Marlborough reviewed his troops in the presence of the Prince, who was much surprised at their smartness after the long march.

"I have heard much of the English cavalry," he said, "and find it indeed to be the best appointed and finest I have ever seen. Money, of which you have no want in England, can buy clothes and arms, but nothing can purchase the spirit which I see in the looks of your men."

"My troops," answered Marlborough, "are now inspirited by your presence. To you we owe that spirit which awakens your admiration."

It was only now after the Neckar had been crossed, and Marlborough had struck through the heart of Germany towards the Danube, that his plans unfolded themselves before the eyes of the world. He would defeat the French before they reached Vienna. He now joined the Imperial German army under the Prince of Baden.

"I am come to meet the deliverer of the Empire," said the Prince.

"I am come to learn of your Highness how to save the Empire," answered Marlborough, though he wrote to his wife a few days later, "You know I am not good at compliments."

They had now reached the Danube. Behind a

little stream which ran through the swampy
ground to the Danube lay the huge army of
French and Bavarians. They were strongly en-
trenched, for in front lay a swamp, to the right
the Danube, to the left some hill country. It
was near the little village of Blenheim, which has
given its name to one of the most memorable
battles in the history of the world. Fifty thousand soldiers in this position feared no foe.

"I know the danger," said Marlborough, when
the officers ventured to suggest the hopelessness
of fighting such an army; "but a battle is ab-
solutely necessary."

He gave orders for a general engagement on the
following day. That anxious night, on the banks
of the fast-flowing Danube, was spent by Marlborough in prayer. He felt a nation's fate hung in
the balance; but "I have great reason to hope that
everything will go well," he wrote calmly home.

The morning of August 13 broke, and the troops
were soon astir; but it was not till midday that
the actual action began. Marlborough himself
chose the centre for his attack. He made an
artificial road across the swamp and threw his
8000 horsemen across. Two of these desperate
charges, led by the Duke himself, decided the day.
The French were flung back on the Danube and
at last forced to surrender. Hundreds were
drowned while trying to swim across the swift
river, 12,000 were slain, 14,000 taken prisoners.

The battle was hardly won when Marlborough took from his pocket-book a slip of paper.

"I have not time to say more," he scribbled to his wife, "but to beg you will give my duty to the Queen, and let her know that her army has had a glorious victory."

This little time-worn note may still be seen at the palace at Blenheim, near Oxford, which was afterwards built at the country's expense for Marlborough, as a memorial of his famous victory.

Not only England, but the whole of Europe, was amazed at the victory at Blenheim. The invincible power of France had at last been checked. The finest French regiments had been destroyed in a single battle. Marlborough had fought with the fate of Europe in his hand and had won. In England his name was on every lip, his praises were sung by poets and statesmen; but in France Louis loved not the name of Marlborough, and the little French children trembled with fear at the sound.

48. HOW PETER THE GREAT LEARNED SHIPBUILDING.

"Nothing can be small to a great man."—JOUKOVSKI.

ONE day in the year 1697, when William III. was yet ruling over England and Holland, the Dutch shipbuilders at the little village of Zaandam were surprised to hear that Peter the Great, Emperor or Tsar of Russia, was at the village inn.

"Yes," said the people, he had come to learn from the Dutch how to build ships, and he was disguised as a common sailor like themselves.

It was quite true. Peter the Great had come from the heart of his great country, Russia; he had crossed the Baltic into Sweden, and thence had reached Holland. It was but six o'clock in the morning when he arrived at Zaandam, and he had been the first to jump ashore and moor his ship to the quay. Meeting a Dutch workman, who had been employed once in Russia, he insisted on going to his cottage for a lodging. It was a small bare cottage built of wood. It had but one room, with a big chimney-corner and a wooden cupboard in which a mattress was laid for sleeping.

"We are only foreign craftsmen seeking work," he told the curious people. Then he bought himself a set of carpenter's tools, carried them to the cottage with his own hands, and set to work at once. He dressed in a Dutch suit, like the local boatmen, in a red waistcoat with large buttons, short jacket, and wide breeches. He spent hours daily watching the shipbuilders at work; he visited saw-mills, oil- and paper-mills, rope-works, sail-makers' and iron-smiths' workshops. He made a model windmill too. He also bought a small ship, made a mast with his own hands, fitted it up, and sailed about the bay.

But meanwhile the news had leaked out that the tall, handsome man, with long curling hair, in the dress of a Dutch sailor, was indeed the Tsar of Russia, and crowds of people began to follow him everywhere. So a week later he escaped to Amsterdam in a violent storm of wind, and there he was given a lodging in the great dockyards of the East India Company. Here he worked steadily for four months, so that he might help in the building of one ship from end to end. He rose early, lit his own fire, cooked his own food, and lived altogether like a simple workman.

It was a very different life to that he had lived in Russia. From his earliest years he had been surrounded with every luxury. As a baby he had slept in a cradle covered with velvet and embroidered with gold, his sheets had been of silk, his frocks of satin trimmed with pearls and emeralds. At three years old he had driven in a little golden carriage drawn by four tiny ponies, while dwarfs rode beside him as bodyguard. As a boy he loved sailors and soldiers, and was enthusiastic about ships and the sea. Such was the boyhood of the man who was to found Russia's army and navy.

Peter the Great was working away in the dockyard at Amsterdam, when one day the Duke of Marlborough visited the docks to see him at work.

Peter the Great at Amsterdam.

"Peter, carpenter of Zaandam, help those men to carry that wood," cried the foreman, in order to point him out to the Englishman. And the Tsar Peter obeyed at once.

When the ship was finished, it was offered to Peter the Great as a present from the city of Amsterdam. He accepted it with joy, christened it the Amsterdam, and carried it back to Russia. He had built his ship, but still he was dissatisfied. He thought the Dutch worked too much by "rule of thumb," that they had no knowledge of ship-building really. So he grew sad and out of spirits; he had travelled so far and had not "reached the desired goal."

"You should come over to England," said an Englishman who was present. "In our country shipbuilding is carried to the highest perfection."

Peter the Great was delighted with the idea. He had met William of Orange, and the King of England had sent him a beautiful ship, constructed on a new plan. Peter now asked him if he might come to England in order to visit the dockyards. William replied by sending over two large ships to conduct the Tsar to England. Arrived in London, Peter the Great went over the large docks at the mouth of the river Thames. He soon mastered the higher branches of ship-building to his satisfaction.

"I should have remained a carpenter only had I not come to England," he used to say afterwards.

But it would take too long to tell how Peter the Great returned to Russia and taught his people how to build ships, how he built the great city which bears his name, Petersburg, to this day. He built it on the shores of the Baltic, at the mouth of a large river, in imitation of Amsterdam, and made it the capital of Russia.

But the story of how he learnt to build ships in Holland and England shows how, in the eyes of the world, those two nations were in advance of all others in the art of shipbuilding.

49. CHARLES XII. OF SWEDEN.

"He left a name, at which the world grew pale,
To point a moral or adorn a tale."
—JOHNSON.

RUSSIA—the largest State in Europe—took no part in public affairs. She lay unheeded amid the snow and ice of her northern clime, until Peter the Great made her mighty enough to play her part in the world's history.

Sweden, on the other hand, had already made her mark. Under Gustavus Adolphus, the Lion of the North, she had become a power among the States of Europe. How she lost everything under Charles XII., and how Russia rose to fame, is one of the most romantic stories in history. Born in 1682, Charles of Sweden was ten years younger than his rival, Peter the Great of Russia.

He early showed signs of future greatness. At
four years old he could perform military exercises
on his pony, at seven he shot his first fox, at
eleven his first bear. He loved stories of war.
His hero in history was Alexander the Great.[1]
He would like to be such a man, he would say.

"But he only lived thirty-two years," said his
tutor.

"One has lived long enough when one has conquered a whole kingdom," answered the boy with a
wisdom beyond his years.

His father, the king, died in 1697, leaving
Sweden at the height of her power. Charles was
a tall, thin boy of fifteen when he was crowned.
It was Christmas time, and the snow fell heavily.
A story says that as the boy-king sprang on
his horse, sceptre in hand, the crown fell off his
head into the snow. A dull murmur went through
the crowd. It was an evil omen.

While Peter the Great was learning shipbuilding
in Holland, Charles was learning to endure hardships bravely. He would get up at night and
lie on bare planks with no clothes over him; for
three nights running he slept in the stables with
no covering but hay. But the moment came when
the boy should suddenly become a man. He was
bear-hunting one day when the news arrived that
the King of Poland had invaded his dominions.

"We will soon make King Augustus return by

---

[1] See Book I. chapter 37.

the way he came," said Charles calmly, turning with a smile to the messenger.

He hurried to his capital, Stockholm, to prepare for war, only to learn that Russia was in league with Poland. His coolness in the face of danger filled every one with surprise.

"I have resolved," he said, "never to begin an unrighteous war, but I have also resolved never to finish a righteous war till I have utterly crushed my enemies."

He left Stockholm, never to return. Peter the Great had besieged a town on the shores of the Baltic, and thither Charles marched with a force of 14,000 Swedes to drive back the Russians. As the boy-king led his troops towards the enemy's lines the sky became dark with a sudden storm ; heavy snow fell, which was driven by the wind into the faces of the Russians. Charles saw his advantage, and advanced rapidly. The Russians were not used to warfare. Their Tsar Peter was serving as a soldier among them, to teach them what he himself had learned ; but he could not stay them in the face of the Swedes, and they fell back in confusion. So Charles gained the victory and entered Narva in triumph. It was but the first of many victories. The youthful conqueror now marched against the King of Poland, with the result that in 1707 the king had formally to resign his crown, which was at once offered to Charles XII., King of Sweden.

The eyes of all Europe were now fixed on this Swedish hero, who was carrying all before him.

Marlborough rushed over to interview Charles in person, and to find out whether he had intentions of joining France; but he noted how the young king's face kindled on mention of Peter the Great, and how the table was strewn with maps of Russia. Charles cared nothing for Europe's wars so long as he could overthrow his rival in Russia.

At last the longed-for moment came, and Charles XII. at the head of a huge army marched into Russia, hoping to reach Moscow in time to deal a deadly blow to the Russians. He was making his way thither when a terrible frost, the like of which had not been known for many years, froze all Europe. Birds dropped dead from the trees; men who fell asleep were frozen to death. Nowhere was it more terrible than in Russia. The sufferings of the Swedes were intense. Yet the king's plans had to be carried out and the daily march made. Thousands perished in the snow, and the situation of the Swedish army became alarming. Supplies were running short, and all communication with Central Europe was now cut off by the Russians.

Since the days of Narva, nine years before, the whole of Russia had awakened. Peter the Great had retaken Narva and built his city of Petersburg. He had built a navy and taught his people modern warfare. So in the spring of

the year 1709 he was ready with a magnificent
army, fresh and well supplied, for the invasion of
Charles. At the head of his troops he now forced
the Swedish king to give battle under the walls
of Pultowa, a fortress to the south of Moscow.

A fresh misfortune now befell the Swedes.
Charles was riding within range of the enemy's
fire when a bullet struck him in the foot. He did
not flinch, but blood dropping fast from his boot,
and his own ghastly paleness, revealed the truth.
In great pain he spent another hour in the trenches
giving orders, until his foot became so swollen
that his boot had to be cut off. Bones were
broken, and the splinters had to be cut away, the
king assisting with a knife himself. But he could
no longer retain the command.

The day of battle dawned, and Charles put on
his uniform, wore a spurred boot on the sound foot,
and placed himself in a litter to be drawn to the
scene of action. The Swedes, whose uniforms were
ragged from their long campaigns, tied a wisp of
straw in their caps and adopted as their watchword " With God's help." Never was Charles more
wanted to command his forces than to-day. The
Swedes fought fearlessly; but the Russian host
was too strong for them, and before evening fell
Peter the Great stood victorious on the field of
Pultowa. Charles, whose litter had been smashed
by a cannon-ball, was borne out of the battle by
his soldiers.

When the Swedish officers surrendered their arms to the Tsar, he asked the commander how he dared to invade a great empire like Russia with a mere handful of men.

"Because the king commanded it," was the loyal answer, "and it is the first duty of a loyal subject to obey his king."

"You are an honest fellow," answered Peter the Great, "and for your loyalty I return you your sword."

Thus Peter triumphed over Sweden.

"The foundations of St Petersburg are firm at last," he cried joyously as the defeated Swedes hastened away from his inhospitable country.

50. THE BOYHOOD OF FREDERICK THE GREAT.

"One of the greatest soldiers ever born."—CARLYLE.

THE battle of Pultowa was over. Peter the Great, the Father of his country, Emperor of Russia, had raised his land to a higher rank in Europe.

Another king was now to arise, the king of a country bordering on Russia, who was to raise his country too, to play her part in the world's history. This was Frederick the Great of Prussia. He was born in 1712, five years after Pultowa, at the Palace of Berlin, capital of the kingdom of Prussia.

He was christened Frederick amid great rejoic-
ings, for two little princes had already died—one
killed by the noise of the cannon fired for joy
over him, the other crushed to death by the
weighty dress and metal crown in which he was
arrayed for his christening.   Little Fritz was
brought up by his father with Spartan severity.
His food was very plain, for his father meant to
make a soldier of him.

"The Prince must from his youth upwards be
trained as officer and general, and to seek all his
glory in the soldier's profession," the king used to
say.   A company of 100 boy-soldiers was formed
for him, and he was drilled to take command of
them, dressed in the Prussian uniform of light
blue and a cocked hat.   But the boy did not
take kindly to soldiering, and no one could guess
at this time that he would one day be a great
soldier.   By the time he was ten years old every
moment had been planned out for him by his
father.

"Every day Fritz is to be called at six, and
rise at once.   You are to stand to him, that he
do not loiter or turn in bed, but briskly and at
once do get up and say his prayers.   This done,
he shall as rapidly as possible get on his shoes,
wash his face and hands, put on a short dressing-
gown, and have his hair combed out.   Whilst
getting combed, he shall at the same time take
breakfast of tea, so that both jobs go on at once,

and this shall be ended before half-past six. From
seven to nine he learns history, from nine to eleven
the Christian religion. Then Fritz rapidly washes
his face with water, hands with soap and water,
puts on clean shirt and coat, and comes to the
king."

The rest of the day is mapped out in the same
style. But under it Fritz grew self-willed. He
refused to have his hair cut according to army
regulations; he "combed it out like a cockatoo,"
which enraged his father, — until one day the
Court surgeon was sent with comb and scissors
and orders to crop the Prince's hair at once. Daily
the little Prince grew more out of favour. In vain
his mother pleaded for him.

"I cannot bear him," cried the angry king.
"He is shy, he cannot ride or shoot, he is not
clean in his person, frizzes his hair like a fool.
All this I have reproved a thousand times, but
in vain."

Still Fritz kept his own way. One day the
king found him playing the flute in a gold-
brocaded dressing-gown. After storming angrily
for some time at the unhappy Prince, he ordered
both dressing-gown and books to be burned.

"Fritz is a piper and a poet," he cried desper-
ately. "He cares nothing for soldiering, and will
undo all that I have been doing."

At last the day came when he could not meet
Fritz without seizing him by the collar and beating

him. The Prince was now eighteen, and his position was unbearable.

"I am in the uttermost despair," he wrote to
his mother; "the king has entirely forgotten that
I am his son. I am driven to extremity. No
longer can I endure such treatment, my patience
is at an end. I go and do not return. I shall
get across to England. Farewell!"

His sister Wilhelmina urged him to give up his
wild plans, but he would not. His escape, how-
ever, was badly planned; he was arrested and
brought back.

"Why did you run away?" roared his father.

"Because you have not treated me as your son,
but as a slave," was the answer.

Then the furious king drew his sword and would
have made an end of his son, had he not been
stopped by an old general.

"Stab me," he cried, "but spare your son."

The Prince was now sent away to a fortress
some sixty miles from Berlin, and lodged in a bare,
strong room alone. His sword was taken from
him. He was dressed in brown prison clothes and
fed on cheap food. His room was opened three
times a-day for four minutes at a time. Lights
were put out at seven. He had no books, no
flute to pass the dreary hours away. He became
melancholy and ill, and the king was besought to
have pity on him lest he should die.

At the end of a year the king thought fit to

visit him. The Prince fell at his father's feet in an agony of grief, which touched even the stony-hearted king.

He was received home again, put back into the army, and slowly won the love and affection of his father.

"I have always loved you," said the king as he lay dying, "though I have been strict with you. God is very good to give me so excellent and worthy a son."

Fritz, with falling tears, kissed his father's hand. The king clasped him in his arms, sobbing, "O my God, I die content since I have such a worthy son and successor."

This was in the year 1740. Much was to happen yet before Frederick the Great succeeded in making Prussia powerful enough to play her own part in the history of Europe.

51. ANSON'S VOYAGE ROUND THE WORLD.

> "Stay, traveller, awhile and view
>   One who has travell'd more than you ;
>   Quite round the globe, through each degree,
>   Anson and I have plough'd the sea."
>   —A. COWLEY.

THE story of Lord Anson's famous voyage in the Centurion, and his capture of the great Spanish treasure-ship, is one of the finest records of the sea.

Frederick the Great had just ascended the throne of Prussia when Anson started off on his expedition against the Spaniards. England and Spain had once more been quarrelling over their trading rights in America, and matters were brought to a crisis by an episode known as "Jenkins's ear." One day an English merchant captain, called Jenkins, told a story in London of how he had been tortured by the Spaniards. He produced from a little box a human ear, which he declared the Spaniards had cut off and bid him take to the English king. England was furious at this insult, and war became inevitable.

George Anson, captain of the ship Centurion, was now appointed to command an expedition bound for the East India Islands by way of South America, with orders to ravage the coast of Peru, capture the Spanish treasure-ships sailing from Mexico, and repeat as far as possible the dashing exploits of Hawkins and Drake [1] a hundred and sixty years before.

The expedition met with delays in starting. It was difficult to get sailors and soldiers for the enterprise, which had to be kept as secret as possible. At last 500 old and infirm soldiers were told off for service under Anson : some were over seventy years of age, some were cripples. The unhappy invalids were unwilling to go, and "all who had limbs and strength to walk away, deserted."

[1] See Book III. chapter 16.

Thus handicapped from the start, Anson at last set out on his "ill-fated but splendid voyage." The year was far advanced, and they were so delayed by winter storms and gales that they took forty days to reach Madeira, a voyage now performed in four days. It was March before they reached the south of America. No longer were the Straits, where Magellan [1] and Drake had encountered such terrific storms, the acknowledged sea-route to the Pacific Ocean. Ships now sailed round Cape Horn, at the extreme south of the island known as Tierra del Fuego, the Land of Fire. The weather was now pleasant, and thinking the worst was over, Anson cheered himself by planning his raid on the Spanish treasure-ships. But no sooner had they reached the extreme south than a tremendous storm of wind, accompanied by hail and rain, broke over the little fleet.

"Never were fiercer seas or blacker skies more cruelly edged with sleet and ice. The very sails were frozen. The rigging was turned into mere ladders of ice. The decks were slippery as glass, and the great seas dashed over them incessantly. The groaning and overstrained ships let in water in every seam, and for over fifty days each furious gale was followed by one yet more furious."

It was a desperate time of year to attempt such a dangerous passage, and it was a wonder that any of the little ships escaped complete destruction.

[1] See Book II. chapter 42.

As it was, after two months of battling with wind and waves, the Centurion found herself alone on the Pacific Ocean. Still there was no peace. Strong westerly gales raged day after day, till the long narrow coast of Chili became "one mad tumult of foam." The skies were dark and black, and when from time to time a glimmer of light made its way through the darkness, it was only to show the heights of the Andes white with snow.

And now a fresh trouble arose. Scurvy broke out among the crew. The legs and arms of the men broke out into open sores, old wounds broke out afresh. They died at the rate of five and six a-day, until 200 had found their last rest under the stormy sea. Still storm upon storm broke over the now half-wrecked ship, full of sick and dying men, until at last the Centurion and two battered ships — all that was left of the fleet that had started—found a long-sought shelter in the harbour of the island of Juan Fernandez, off the southern coast of America. Of the 961 men who had sailed from England, only 335 were left alive. How could such as these ever hope to capture Spanish treasure-ships? But the brave heart of Anson was undaunted ; each fresh disaster made him only more determined to succeed.

After a stay of 130 days on the island for repairs and refreshment, he set sail for the coast of Chili and Peru. How he captured the Spanish town of

Paita at dead of night with only sixty British sailors, and carried off the silver from the treasury, is a story unsurpassed in naval history. Sailing on past Panama, he next laid wait off Acapulco for one of the great Mexican treasure-ships, but the Spaniards caught sight of an English sail in the distance, and they kept their treasure-ships at home. Had not the fight of Sir Richard Grenville [1] on the little Revenge taught them to beware of the Englishman at sea?

It was no use waiting there any longer, so Anson turned his ships and faced the trackless path of the lonely Pacific Ocean. It was now May 1742. Two ships were left him now, and a furious gale disabled one; so the Centurion alone, with her great figurehead of a huge lion rampant carved in wood, ploughed the merciless waves of the wide Pacific. Scurvy was again doing its work and carrying off the crew by scores. Food was bad, water scarce; but for three months Anson resolutely kept on his way until the Ladrone Islands were reached. He was now down with scurvy himself, but pure water and fresh fruits soon revived the drooping men, and onwards they sailed once more.

It was now two years since he had left England, —years of hardship and suffering, of heroism unshaken by plague or storm. But his orders were yet unfulfilled. A treasure-ship from Mexico was

[1] See Book III. chapter 21.

due at the Philippine Islands on its way home
to Spain. It would be a "stout ship and fully
manned," probably with a crew of 600. Anson's
crew was now 201. Should they try and capture
her? With a shout of joy the stout - hearted
sailors expressed their willingness to do or die.
It was early dawn, one morning in June, when a
cry rang through the silent air, "The ship! the
ship!"

The Spanish vessel bore in sight, and the
little Centurion sailed quickly towards her. In
a squall of wind and rain Anson attacked her
while she was yet totally unprepared. He scourged
the Spanish decks with fire and drove the men
from their guns. Soon he had captured his prize.
With a mere handful of men, for he lost 150 killed
and wounded, he navigated his own ship and the
Spanish galleon through dangerous and unknown
seas, he rounded the Cape of Good Hope, and
landed in England on June 15, 1744, with his
treasure. His voyage had been yet more amazing
than that of Drake 160 years before. Amid un-
rivalled disaster Anson had brought his ship right
round the world, he had fulfilled his orders, and he
had added enduring fame to the British flag.

52. MARIA THERESA.

"Fair Austria spreads her mournful charms,
The Queen—the beauty, sets the world in arms."
—DR JOHNSON.

ANSON returned home to find that during his four
years' absence Europe had plunged into a terrible
war. He had but just started when the Emperor
of Austria died somewhat unexpectedly. He had
left his crown and all his vast possessions to his
eldest daughter, Maria Theresa. The story of this
young and beautiful queen, left at the age of
twenty - three to rule over the large empire of
Austria, is a stirring one in the world's history.

She was born at Vienna in 1717, and was "the
prettiest little maiden in the world," when Frederick
the Great was beginning his unhappy childhood at
Berlin. When she was but seven years old, her
father made up his mind that she should succeed
him if he had no son. He drew up a great
document, known to history as the "Pragmatic
Sanction." It was accepted by Spain, England, Prussia, Russia, and Holland, and refused by
France and Bavaria. The little Maria Theresa was
brought up as the future Empress of Austria.
At the age of fourteen she was admitted to council
meetings, and she listened with eager interest to
all she could understand. People often took ad-

vantage of the little girl, giving her petitions to carry to her father till he became angry with her.

"You seem to think that a sovereign has nothing to do but to grant favours," he said at last.

"I see nothing else that can make a crown bearable," answered the child.

She insisted on learning the history and geography of her own country, and ever tried to fit herself for the high position she was some day to take. One story says that a marriage between Maria Theresa and Frederick the Great was planned, which might have altered the whole course of European history. A marriage with the Spanish heir was certainly talked of, but Maria Theresa, with tears, insisted on marrying her cousin, the Duke of Lorraine. She had been married four years when her father died. Maria Theresa suddenly found herself Empress of Austria, Queen of Hungary and Bohemia, and Sovereign of the Netherlands. She reigned over some of the finest and fairest provinces of Europe; over nations speaking different languages, governed by different laws, and held together by no link save that of acknowledging the same queen. That queen was very young and very beautiful, but quite inexperienced.

Within a few months her right to these provinces was questioned, and Europe began to grab her outlying possessions. France, Spain, and Prussia led the way. England and Holland remained true to their promise. Like a hind in the forest when the hunters are abroad and the fiercely baying hounds are on every side, so stood the lovely Queen Maria Theresa. She trembled for the safety of her empire, not knowing from which side the fury of the chase would burst upon her. She was determined to yield nothing.

"The inheritance which my father has left me, we will not part with these. Death, if it must be, but not dishonour."

Her helpless condition excited the greatest pity in England, and King George II. came over in person to fight for her. But before he came over to help, Frederick the Great had already claimed Silesia. One snowy day in April 1741, he fought a great battle against the Austrians, and all Europe from this time seemed to break into war. In the midst of these distresses a son and heir was born, and called Joseph.

After this, and amid scenes of the greatest enthusiasm, Maria Theresa was crowned Queen of Hungary. Presburg, the old capital, was some fifty miles from Vienna. Here the old iron crown of Hungary was placed upon her head, a sacred robe was thrown over her, a sword was girded to her side. Thus dressed, she mounted a splendid horse, and riding to a piece of rising ground she drew her sword, and, waving it towards the four quarters of the globe, she seemed to be defying war and "conquering all who saw her."

The crown had never been placed on so small a head before ; it had been lined with cushions to make it fit. But it was heavy and hot, and when the young queen sat down to dine in the great hall of the castle after the coronation, she begged to have it taken off. As it was removed, her beautiful hair, no longer confined, fell in long ringlets on her shoulders. It is said that her Hungarian nobles could hardly keep from shouting applause.

Three months later, at this very Presburg, one of the most famous scenes in history took place, when Maria Theresa threw herself and her infant son upon the mercy of these very Hungarian nobles.

Her enemies had now reached the very gates of Vienna, and, taking the six-month-old baby, she was obliged to flee for her life, leaving her husband to maintain her cause. Making her way to her old capital, she summoned the Hungarians to a great meeting in the castle. It was September 11, 1741, a day ever remembered in the annals of Hungary. The great hall was already full when the young queen entered. She was in deep mourning, for it was not yet a year since her father had died. Her dress was Hungarian, the iron crown was on her head, the sword of state in her hand. Though her step was firm, her tears were falling fast, and for some time after she had ascended the throne she was unable to speak.

For some moments there was deep silence. Then a statesman rose and explained the melancholy position to which the queen was reduced.

Maria Theresa had now recovered herself. On a cushion before her lay her baby son Joseph, afterwards Emperor of Austria. The queen now took him in her arms. She held him up to the assembly before her. Her face, still wet with tears, was "beautiful as the moon riding among wet, stormy clouds." She spoke in Latin, the official language of Hungary to this day.

"The kingdom of Hungary, our person, our children, our crowns, are at stake," she cried to them amidst her sobs. "Forsaken by all, we seek shelter only in the tried fidelity, the arms, the well-known valour of the Hungarians."

The beauty and distress of their unhappy queen roused every Hungarian to the wildest enthusiasm. Each man drew his sword, and all cried as with one voice, which re-echoed through the lofty hall, "Our lives, our blood for your Majesty! We will die for our *king*, Maria Theresa!"

The young queen burst into tears.

"We wept too," said one of the nobles present; "but they were tears of pity, admiration, and fury."

From this day matters improved. It is true the province of Silesia was lost; but through the long wars that characterised the reign, other provinces were added to Austria.

And so the queen played her difficult part, and

played it well. She was succeeded on the throne
by her son Joseph, while her youngest daughter,
Marie Antoinette,[1] became the wife of the French
Dauphin, of whom we shall hear presently.

53. THE STORY OF SCOTLAND.

"Land of the mountain and the flood."—SCOTT.

EUROPE was busily engaged in warfare. George
II. of England had but just returned from the
Continent, where he had been helping Maria
Theresa against her many foes, when suddenly
the news rang through England that another of
the hapless Stuarts was in arms in Scotland.

Let us take a glance at this Scotland, this

"Land of the mountain and the flood,"

which together with England and Wales is known
as Great Britain. Unlike the sister country, Ireland, no salt waves of the sea divide her from
England ; only the Cheviot Hills separate the two
countries, which have been united since the year
1603.

"One life, one flag, one fleet, one throne."

It is the most mountainous part of Great Britain,
and this fact has had a great deal to do with the
story of Scotland and the character of her people.

[1] See Book IV. chapter 14.

There are the Highlands and the Lowlands, the Highlanders and the Lowlanders.

The union of England and Scotland under one king took place in 1603. In that year Elizabeth of England lay dying, leaving no child to succeed her on the English throne. In vain she had been begged to name an heir. As death approached she spoke constantly of James, King of Scotland, now a man of thirty - six. Again the courtiers pressed her to name her heir.

"My seat," she murmured, "hath been the seat of kings, and I will have no rascal to succeed me."

Once more they pressed her for a name.

"And who should it be," she whispered with her last breath, "but our cousin of Scotland?"

So James was crowned King of England, Scotland, and Ireland, assuming the title of King of Great Britain. Mutual advantage arose to both countries, former discords were soon forgotten, while the poets burst into triumphant songs over the union :—

> "The flag of their union far o'er the wide earth
> Is welcomed with gladness; and ne'er may it cease
> To wave as the emblem of valour and worth,
> Proclaiming in battle the promise of peace.
> The children shall equal the deeds of the sire,
> The future in glory out-glory the past;
> And dearly we'll cherish, till time shall expire,
> One Country, one Cause, and one Hope at the last."

From the death of James I. the Scottish people took up the cause of the Stuarts.

And so it was that in the year 1745, when the exiled grandson of James landed in the Hebrides, the clans with one accord rallied to his standard at Glenfinnan,—

> "When the mighty heart of Scotland, all too big to slumber more,
> Burst in wrath and exultation, like a huge volcano's roar."

His force swelled as he marched in triumph to Edinburgh to proclaim his father, the "Old Pretender," king. Two thousand English troops sent against him were cut to pieces in a single charge of furious clansmen at Prestonpans in the course of ten minutes. Victory doubled the Scottish forces, and the Young Pretender, as he was now called, was at the head of 6000 Highlanders. Matters were growing serious, when George II. of England sent his second son, the Duke of Cumberland, against the Highland troops under the Young Pretender.

The armies met at Culloden Moor, near Inverness. The English army was large, well fed, well trained— a contrast to the Highland troops under the Prince, who had eaten but a biscuit each the day before the battle. The Prince was desperate. He planned a night march as his only hope of defeating such an army. Setting the heath on fire, to convey the idea that the Highland troops were camping for the night, Prince Charlie set forth with his men in profound silence. The night was very dark and progress was slow. At two o'clock in the

morning they were yet four miles from the English
camp. A distant roll of guns told them that the
English were not asleep. It was useless to risk
a surprise. Instead, the Highlanders crowned the
heights of Culloden. They were now tired, foot-
sore, weary, having passed the night in marching.
They were also without food. They lay down to
snatch a few hours' sleep, when a sudden alarm
announced the English army. Hurry and confusion
reigned, but the clansmen soon flung themselves
in a wild rush on the English. They were received with a terrible fire of musketry by the
troops under the Duke of Cumberland. All that
courage and despair could do was done. There
was the howl of the Highland advance, the scream
of the onset, the thunder of musketry, the din of
trumpet and drum, the flash of firearms, the glitter
of broadswords. And then came the end. The
battle was over as rapidly as all other Highland
conflicts. Soon, very soon, the Highland force was
fleeing from the field, away from the field of
Culloden, never to be banded more in the hopeless cause of the Stuarts.

Culloden was over and Prince Charlie a fugitive.
Attended by a faithful few, he embarked in an
open boat for the Hebrides. A violent storm
arose, rain poured down in torrents, vivid lightning showed the blackness of the raging waters,
while thunder crashed overhead.

Meanwhile a heavy price was set on his head.

Search-parties were everywhere, and he had many a narrow escape of falling into the hands of his enemies. When he reached Stornoway at last, he was drenched to the skin and had tasted no food for eighteen hours. A faithful friend took pity on him and gave him food and shelter. For many a long day the little band sailed about among the creeks and islands of the Outer Hebrides, now chased by a man-of-war, now driven on to the desolate rocks by the fury of the sea, eating oatmeal mixed with salt water as an alternative to starvation. For every creek and ferry along those wild shores was watched by English soldiers. There was £30,000 for the man who would give up Prince Charlie. And not a man was found to betray his Prince. Many were the songs written and sung about this Scottish idol—this Prince Charlie of Scottish romance.

It is a well-known story how the Prince fell into the hands of Flora Macdonald, and how she planned his escape to the island of Skye. She dressed him as her tall Irish maid Betty Burke, in a flowered print gown and quilted petticoat, white apron, cloak, and hood. As such he accompanied her to the sea-shore, though boats of armed men were watching them at the time. Under cover of darkness they sailed across the stormy waters to Skye.

> " ' Speed, bonnie boat, like a bird on the wing,
> Onward,' the sailors cry ;
> ' Carry the lad that's born to be King
> Over the sea to Skye.' "

But there was danger here too. The Prince was tall.

"What long strides the maid takes, and how awkwardly she manages her petticoats!" said a bystander, and the Prince had to change his dress.

So he wandered about from place to place, and the faithful Highlanders kept their secret bravely, till finally the Prince made his way to France.

Thus ended the last attempt of the unlucky Stuarts to regain the crown of Scotland and England. George II. was firmly established on the throne of Great Britain and Ireland, and his direct descendants still rule over the ever-increasing Empire.

TEACHER'S APPENDIX.

Chap.
1. *Dutch Republic.* Motley.
   General Sketch of European History. Freeman.
   Holland. Rogers. Story of the Nations.
4. Short History of the English People. *The New Learning.* Green.
   Erasmus. Emerton. Heroes of the Reformation.
5. *Martin Luther.* Jacobs. Heroes of the Reformation.
   Luther. Carlyle's *Heroes and Hero-Worship.*
7. *Dutch Republic.* Motley.
10. *William the Silent.* F. Harrison. Foreign Statesmen.
11. *Henry of Navarre and the Huguenots in France.* Willert. Heroes of the
    Nations.
   History of France. Vol. ii. Kitchin.
14. *Students' History of England.* Vol. ii. S. Gardiner.
   Short History of the English People. Green.
15. *The Age of Elizabeth.* Creighton. Epochs of Modern History.
   English Seamen in the Sixteenth Century. Froude.
16. *Life of Drake.* Corbett. English Men of Action.
17. *The Armada.* Macaulay's Lays.
   Students' History of England. S. Gardiner.
   Short History of the English People. Green.
   Short Studies on Great Subjects. Froude.
   Westward Ho! (Fiction.) Kingsley.
18. *Short Studies on Great Subjects.* Froude. England's Forgotten Worthies.
19. *Sir Humphrey Gilbert.* (Poem.) Longfellow.
   America. Doyle. Macmillan's Historical Course.
20. *Life of Sir Walter Raleigh.* M. Hume. Builders of Greater Britain.
   Raleigh and his Times. Vol. i. Kingsley's Miscellanies.
21. *The Revenge.* (Poem.) Tennyson.
22. *Discovery of Guiana.* Raleigh. (Cassell's National Library, 3d.)
23. *The Fairy Queen.* (Poem.) Spenser.
   St George and the Dragon, in Penny Poets' edition, No. 18.
   Life of Spenser. Church. English Men of Letters.
24. *Shakspere.* Primer. Dowden. Ed. J. R. Green.
   Merchant of Venice. (Play.) Shakspere.
   Shakspere. Carlyle's *Heroes and Hero-Worship.*
25. *Life of Elizabeth.* Beesly. Twelve English Statesmen.
   See also *The Building of the Empire.* The Story of England's Growth
    from Elizabeth to Victoria. Vol. i.
   The Puritan Revolution. (1603-1660.) S. Gardiner. Epochs of Modern
    History.

Chap.
26. *John Davis, the Navigator.* Markham. The World's Great Explorers.
29. *Story of Canada.* Kennedy. Empire Series.
   Canada. Bourinot. Story of the Nations.
30. *The Courtship of Miles Standish.* (Poem.) Longfellow.
   Short History of the English People. Green.
31. *Thirty Years' War.* S. Gardiner. Epochs of Modern History.
   Gustavus Adolphus and the Struggle of Protestantism for Existence. Fletcher. Heroes of the Nations.
33. *Story of Geographical Discovery.* Jacobs.
   Story of Australia. Flora Shaw. Empire Series.
   European Colonies. Payne. Macmillan's Historical Course.
34. *Story of South Africa.* Basil Worsfold. Empire Series.
   South Africa. Theal. Story of the Nations.
35. *Life of Oliver Cromwell.* F. Harrison. Twelve English Statesmen.
   Life of Oliver Cromwell. S. Gardiner.
   See *Sonnet on Cromwell.* Milton.
   English Restoration and Louis XIV. (1648-1679.) Airy. Epochs of Modern History.
36. *Admiral Blake.* Hannay. English Worthies edition. Andrew Lang.
38. *America.* Doyle. Macmillan's Historical Course.
   Short History of the English People. Green.
39. *The Pilgrim's Progress.* John Bunyan.
   Life of Bunyan. Froude. English Men of Letters. Ed. Morley.
40. *William III.* Traill. Twelve English Statesmen.
42. *Ireland.* E. Lawless. Story of the Nations.
44. *Louis XIV. and the Zenith of the French Monarchy.* Hassall. Heroes of the Nations.
   Louis XIV. Wakeman. Foreign Statesmen.
46. *Life of Marlborough.* Saintsbury. English Worthies.
47. *The Battle of Blenheim.* (Poem.) Southey.
   Histories of England as above.
49. *Charles XII. and the Collapse of the Swedish Empire.* (1682-1719.) Nisbet Bain. Heroes of the Nations.
   Charles XII. Voltaire.
50. *Frederick the Great.* Carlyle.
   Frederick the Great and the Seven Years' War. Longman. Epochs of Modern History.
52. *Maria Theresa.* F. Bright. Foreign Statesmen.
53. *Scotland.* Mackintosh. Story of the Nations.

COSIMO is a specialty publisher of books and publications that inspire, inform, and engage readers. Our mission is to offer unique books to niche audiences around the world.

COSIMO BOOKS publishes books and publications for innovative authors, nonprofit organizations, and businesses. **COSIMO BOOKS** specializes in bringing books back into print, publishing new books quickly and effectively, and making these publications available to readers around the world.

COSIMO CLASSICS offers a collection of distinctive titles by the great authors and thinkers throughout the ages. At **COSIMO CLASSICS** timeless works find new life as affordable books, covering a variety of subjects including: Business, Economics, History, Personal Development, Philosophy, Religion & Spirituality, and much more!

COSIMO REPORTS publishes public reports that affect your world, from global trends to the economy, and from health to geopolitics.

FOR MORE INFORMATION CONTACT US AT
INFO@COSIMOBOOKS.COM

❋ if you are a book lover interested in our current catalog of books

❋ if you represent a bookstore, book club, or anyone else interested in special discounts for bulk purchases

❋ if you are an author who wants to get published

❋ if you represent an organization or business seeking to publish books and other publications for your members, donors, or customers.

**COSIMO BOOKS ARE ALWAYS
AVAILABLE AT ONLINE BOOKSTORES**

VISIT COSIMOBOOKS.COM
BE INSPIRED, BE INFORMED